Contents

Introduction

Each page of Maths Express has work on one topic.

First there is a quick introduction to the topic that shows how to do the exercises. There is sometimes a drawing to help you.

Last of all there is a Challenge section. This should be quite difficult and might take longer than the rest of the page. You might need help with some of it.

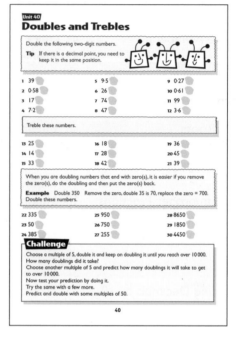

Then there are about 30 questions – your teacher may not want you to do all of them.

The Problem pages have word problems on them.
Read very carefully!

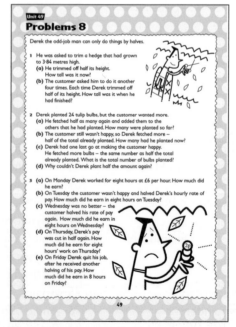

You should do your work in your own book.
Remember to copy the questions carefully.

Working with Large Numbers

The value of each digit in a number is affected by its place: millions, hundred thousands, ten thousands, thousands, hundreds, tens, units. We usually leave a space between every three digits in numbers from 10 000 upwards to make them easier to read (some people use a comma instead). When we read large numbers, we pause when we reach a space.

Write these numbers down in words.

Example   1 542 781: one million, five hundred and forty-two thousand, seven hundred and eighty-one

1 32 561   3 956 029   5 8 306 289   7 10 758 187   9 35 402 654

2 261 869   4 5 464 382   6 6 054 764   8 16 238 063

Sometimes we only need to work to the nearest whole number of 10s, 100s or 1000s. To do this we look at the numeral in the next column to the right. **If it is more than 4, we round up. If it is less than 5, we round down.**

Example   Round 5276 to the nearest 1000. There are 2 hundreds, so we round down.

When rounding up, you may have to exchange to the next column to the left.

Example   Round 65 964 to the nearest 100.   **66 000**

Round these numbers to the nearest 10.

10 578   11 3324   12 5696   13 45 766   14 205 564   15 5 555 555

Round these numbers to the nearest 100.

16 849   18 6563   20 76 498   22 1 574 646   24 55 342 925

17 5731   19 37 739   21 45 962   23 4 867 472

Round these numbers to the nearest 1000.

25 8537   26 34 473   27 59 436   28 427 024   29 4 604 841   30 24 199 264

Challenge

Using the numerals 0, 2, 3, 5, 7, 9, make as many six-digit numbers as you can. Rearrange them into ascending order (starting with the lowest) and descending order (starting with the highest).

Multiplying and Dividing Large Numbers by 10, 100 or 1000

To multiply by 10 you can use a zero to push the digits one column to the left, which makes them worth ten times more.
To multiply by 100 you use two zeros.

Example 47 653 × 10 = **476 530**   47 653 × 100 = **4 765 300**
47 653 × 1000 = 47 653 **000**

To divide by 10 or 100, move the numerals to the right. This might mean using a decimal point. Remove any zeros that are not needed.

Example 2940 ÷ 10 = **2940**   2940 ÷ 100 = **29·40**   2940 ÷ 1000 = **2·94**

1 2464 × 10 =
2 74 456 × 100 =
3 364 225 × 10 =
4 35 240 ÷ 10 =
5 1439 × 1000 =
6 2 682 000 ÷ 1000 =
7 47 600 ÷ 100 =
8 94 430 ÷ 100 =
9 74 702 × 100 =
10 3836 × 1000 =

11 8 432 453 × 10 =
12 1 595 346 × 10 =
13 5 864 351 ÷ 10 =
14 128 830 ÷ 100 =
15 7 409 790 ÷ 10 =
16 684 560 ÷ 100 =
17 65 500 ÷ 1000 =
18 15 408 × 100 =
19 92 247 × 1000 =
20 2 548 650 × 10 =

21 1 900 650 ÷ 1000 =
22 23 580 × 100 =
23 736 055 ÷ 10 =
24 67 245 × 1000 =
25 2 520 609 × 10 =
26 342 600 ÷ 1000 =
27 824 840 ÷ 10 =
28 8 320 000 ÷ 100 =
29 4321 × 1000 =
30 39 685 × 100 =

Challenge

Choose a six-digit number of your own.
Multiply it by 10, multiply the answer by 100, and then multiply that answer by 1000.
How many times will you have to divide your final answer by 10 to get back to the number you started with?
Try again with another number, multiplying by 10, 100, 100, 100 and 1000.
How many times do you have to divide by 100 to get back to your starting number?

Positive and Negative Numbers

We can count back below 0, using **negative numbers**. We put a minus sign in front of them and say **minus 1** and so on.

Numbers larger than 0 are **positive**. We don't need to use a + sign.

Write these sets of number down in order of size, starting with the lowest.

Example $4, -6, 7, 0, -4$ **$-6, -4, 0, 4, 7$**

1 $34, -20, 5, 45, -5$ 4 $0, -1, -6, 6, 8, -10$ 7 $-16, -32, -8, -12$

2 $-7, 6, -12, -15, 12$ 5 $-8, 30, 36, -50, -40$ 8 $-15, 5, -10, 20, -20$

3 $54, -25, -54, 0, 25$ 6 $33, -22, 19, -41, 153$ 9 $42, 24, -24, -42, -22, 22$

Finding the **difference** between two negative numbers is easy with a number line – just count the 'jumps'.

10 $-4, -14$ 11 $-16, -12$ 12 $-8, -16$ 13 $-10, -19$ 14 $-18, -6$ 15 $-7, -20$

Work out these differences **without** using the number line.

16 $-15, -10$ 17 $-25, -20$ 18 $-35, -15$

Finding the difference between a negative number and a positive number is also easy on a number line. You will have to pass the zero as you count on or back.

19 $-5, 10$ 20 $12, -10$ 21 $-20, 15$ 22 $-15, 20$ 23 $20, -20$ 24 $-18, 17$

If we want to find the difference between a positive and a negative number, we find the difference between each number and 0, then add the differences together.

Example $-35, 24$ -35 to 0 is **35** and 0 to 24 is **24**, so the difference is
$35 + 24 = $ **59**

Work out these differences **without** using the number line.

25 $28, -22$ 26 $-17, 54$ 27 $-22, 35$ 28 $24, -32$ 29 $14, -16$ 30 $-6, 34$

Challenge

With a partner, one of you pick ten positive and the other pick ten negative numbers. Put them in pairs and see who can find the differences the fastest **without** using a number line. Repeat with two more sets of negative and positive numbers.

1 The temperature outside Father Christmas's house
is −24° Celsius. Start at this temperature each time.
What will it be if it:
(a) rises 10 degrees
(b) falls 6 degrees
(c) falls 14 degrees
(d) rises 25 degrees
(e) rises 30 degrees
(f) falls 11 degrees?

2 A train is supposed to arrive at the station at
09:00 each morning and leave straight away.
It usually arrives early and leaves late. How long
does it spend in the station if it arrives and
leaves at these times?
(a) Monday: arrives 5 minutes early
and leaves 2 minutes late
(b) Tuesday: arrives 1 minute early
and leaves 3 minutes late
(c) Wednesday: arrives 2 minutes late
and leaves 3 minutes late
(d) Thursday: arrives 3 minutes early
and leaves 4 minutes late
(e) Friday: arrives 6 minutes early
and leaves 1 minute late
(f) Saturday: arrives 8 minutes early
and leaves 1 minute early.

3 Calculate the number of days between these dates:
(a) 4 days before 1st April and 6 days after
(b) 8 days before 16th May and 4 days after
(c) 10 days before 2nd August and 16 days after
(d) 7 days before Christmas Day and 8 days after
(e) 12 days before 1st January and 20 days after.

Number Sequences

Look at the sequences of numbers below·
Write down each sequence, decide what the
pattern is, and then write down the next six numbers.

Example   7, 9, 11, 13,   The numbers are increasing by 2 each time, so
                 7, 9, 11, 13, **15, 17, 19, 21, 23, 25**

1 0, 10, 20, 30,
2 0, 20, 40, 60,
3 180, 160, 140, 120,
4 90, 80, 70, 60,
5 0, 15, 30, 45,

6 135, 120, 105, 90,
7 0, 25, 50, 75,
8 36, 46, 56, 66,
9 225, 200, 175, 150,
10 17, 37, 57, 77,

11 111, 101, 91, 81,
12 334, 314, 294, 274,
13 6, 18, 30, 42,
14 330, 300, 270, 240,
15 114, 102, 90, 78,

Try these sequences, which include decimals.

16 0, 0·2, 0·4, 0·6,
17 2·5, 2·25, 2·0, 1·75,

18 1·8, 1·6, 1·4, 1·2,
19 0, 0·3, 0·6, 0·9,

20 0, 0·25, 0·5, 0·75,
21 2·4, 2·1, 1·8, 1·5,

Copy these sequences and put in the missing numbers.

22 ⬡ ⬡ 35 ⬡ 45 ⬡ 65, ⬡

23 ⬡ 65, 80, ⬡ 110, ⬡ ⬡

24 ⬡ 95, 80, ⬡ 50, ⬡ ⬡

25 490, 440, ⬡ 340, ⬡ ⬡ 190

26 30, ⬡ 70, 90, ⬡ ⬡ ⬡

27 327, 277, 227, ⬡ ⬡ ⬡ ⬡

28 ⬡ 182, ⬡ 122, ⬡ ⬡ ⬡

29 ⬡ 51, ⬡ 101, ⬡ 151, ⬡

30 17, 32, ⬡ 62, ⬡ ⬡ 107

Challenge

Have another look at the sequences in questions 16 to 21.
Make up a decimal number sequence of your own, increasing by less than 1 each time.
Can you reverse the sequence?
Do the same again, starting from a different number but increasing by the same
amount.
Reverse this sequence.
Try some more, increasing and decreasing by a decimal number that is more than
1 (e.g. 1·5).

Odd and Even Numbers

An **even** number of objects can be halved exactly into two **equal** sets.
Halving an **odd** number of objects leaves an **odd one** left over.
Even whole numbers end with 0, 2, 4, 6 or 8 in the units column.
Odd whole numbers end with 1, 3, 5, 7 or 9 in the units column.

1 Sort these numbers into two sets, odd numbers and even numbers:
22, 9, 37, 81, 30, 46, 73, 38.

2 Write down all the odd numbers that come between 50 and 70.

3 Write down all the even numbers that come between 71 and 91.

If you understand odd and even numbers, it is easier to check your answers. In the explanations below, **O** stands for an odd number and **E** stands for an even number.

$O + O = E$ $E + E = E$ $E + O = O$ and $O + E = O$
$O - O = E$ $E - E = E$ $E - O = O$ and $O - E = O$

Complete the following equations and alongside each, copy the correct 'explanation'.

Example $23 + 62$ $23 + 62 = 75, O + E = O$

4 $34 + 56 =$

5 $83 - 46 =$

6 $25 + 42 =$

7 $78 - 31 =$

8 $33 + 67 =$

9 $78 - 56 =$

10 $68 - 47 =$

11 $38 + 48 =$

12 $26 + 32 =$

13 $54 - 28 =$

14 $95 - 47 =$

15 $44 + 39 =$

Odd and even numbers affect the answers when we multiply.

$O \times O = O$ $E \times E = E$ $E \times O = E$ and $O \times E = E$

We only get an odd **product** (answer to a multiplication) when both numbers are odd.
Complete these equations, again copying the correct 'explanation' alongside.

Example 7×6 $7 \times 6 = 42, O \times E = E$

16 $6 \times 8 =$

17 $8 \times 7 =$

18 $5 \times 6 =$

19 $7 \times 9 =$

20 $7 \times 4 =$

21 $3 \times 7 =$

22 $6 \times 9 =$

23 $8 \times 8 =$

24 $4 \times 3 =$

25 $10 \times 5 =$

26 $9 \times 9 =$

27 $9 \times 8 =$

28 $5 \times 7 =$

29 $10 \times 9 =$

30 $4 \times 6 =$

Challenge

Write down some multiplication equations with larger numbers (two or more digits), but don't work out the answers yet.
Use what you have learnt to predict if the answer will be odd or even.
Use a calculator to see if you were correct.

Multiples and Divisibility

When we multiply two numbers, the **product** (the number produced) is a **multiple** of the two numbers. 36 is a multiple of 2, 3, 4, 5, 6, 9, 12 and 18 because $2 \times 18 = 36$, $3 \times 12 = 36$, $4 \times 9 = 36$ and $6 \times 6 = 36$.
Write whether these numbers are multiples of any of 2, 5, 10, 50 or 100.

1 70   2 200   3 320   4 170   5 300   6 75

Write whether these numbers are multiples of any of 3, 4, 6, 7, 8 or 9.

7 60   8 72   9 63   10 99   11 42   12 105

The a**bility** to be **div**ided by another number is called **div**isi**bility**.
If a number is divisible by 2, it must be an **even** number. **If it is divisible by 4**, you must get an **even** number when you **halve** it. **If it is divisible by 5**, it must end in **5** or **0**.
If it is divisible by 10, it must end in **0**. **If it is divisible by 3**, add up the digits – the answer will be **3 or a multiple of 3**. **If it is divisible by 9**, add up the digits – the answer will be **9 or a multiple of 9**.
Write whether these numbers are is divisible by any of 2, 3, 4, 5, 9 or 10.

13 54   15 35   17 170   19 75   21 96
14 28   16 270   18 93   20 34

If a number is divisible by 6, halve it then add up the digits – the answer will be a 3 or a multiple of 3. **If it is divisible by 8**, you must get an **even** number when you **halve** it **twice**. Say if these numbers are divisible by 6, 8, both or neither.

22 120   24 144   26 96   28 160   30 192
23 47   25 69   27 240   29 125

Challenge

Choose some numbers to put into this Carroll diagram.

	is a multiple of 6	is not a multiple of 6
is a multiple of 8		
is not a multiple of 8		

Squares and Square Roots

If we draw a square with 5 rows of 5 smaller squares, we get 25 squares altogether. This is why when we multiply a number by itself, we say that we have **squared** it. We say that 25 is a **square number** because it can be used to make a square.

A shorter way of saying that a number has been squared is to put a small ^{2} after it. $5 \times 5 = 5^2$

We use a ^{2} to mean 'squared' because we have two dimensions in a square, length and width.

Complete these 'squarings'. Ask your teacher if you can use a calculator for questions 11 to 21.

1 $4^2 =$	6 $6^2 =$	11 $0^2 =$	16 $12^2 =$
2 $7^2 =$	7 $1^2 =$	12 $11^2 =$	17 $17^2 =$
3 $2^2 =$	8 $3^2 =$	13 $14^2 =$	18 $13^2 =$
4 $8^2 =$	9 $5^2 =$	14 $19^2 =$	19 $15^2 =$
5 $10^2 =$	10 $9^2 =$	15 $16^2 =$	20 $20^2 =$

With square numbers you can find out where they came from by reversing the process.

We call this finding the **square root**.

Find the square root of these numbers.

21 81	23 36	25 25	27 49	29 9
22 64	24 100	26 4	28 16	30 1

Challenge

Write down the squares of 1, 3, 5, 7 and 9, leaving a space between each number.

Underneath each space write the difference between the numbers.

Underneath this row of 'differences', write the difference between each pair of differences.

1	9	25 ... and so on
8	16 ... and so on	
8 ... and so on		

What do you notice?

Try the same using the squares of even numbers.

Triangular Numbers

When we put objects a triangle shape, we get **triangular numbers**. Each row we add has one more than the previous row. The number of balls in the last row is the same as the number of rows.

1 Draw a set of snooker balls with five rows. How many balls are there altogether?
2 Add a sixth row. How many balls are there now?
3 Add a seventh row. How many balls are there now?

How many snooker balls will there be if there are:

4 8 rows   5 9 rows   6 10 rows?

7 Complete this sequence of triangular numbers. 1, 3, 6, 10, 15, 21, 28,

Below are the triangles of balls that make up some triangular numbers. Add the first and last number, then the second and next-to-last number and so on.

8 1, 2, 3, 4, 5, 6   9 1, 2, 3, 4, 5, 6, 7, 8   10 1, 2, 3, 4, 5, 6, 7, 8, 9, 10

11 Questions 8 to 10 are all even numbers of rows. What do you notice?

Try the same with these odd numbers of rows.

12 1, 2, 3, 4, 5, 6, 7   13 1, 2, 3, 4, 5, 6, 7, 8, 9   14 1, 2, 3, 4, 5, 6, 7, 8, 9, 10, 11

15 What do you notice about the totals and the number left over?

A quick way to find a triangular number is: **add 1 to the number of rows and multiply by half of the number of rows**.

Example   8 rows: $(8 + 1) \times (8 \div 2) = 9 \times 4 = 36$

Use this method to work out the triangular numbers created with these rows.

16 12 rows   17 13 rows   18 14 rows

Challenge

A shopkeeper wants to display tins of beans in a triangular stack. Using a calculator and the above method, work out how many tins he will need to make stacks with 16, 17, 18, 19 and 20 rows. If he had 7 boxes of 24 tins, what is the tallest triangular stack he could make?

Factors and Prime Numbers

A **factor** is any number that is multiplied to make another number.
1, 2, 3, 4, 6, 8, 12, 16, 24 and 48 are all factors of 48 because 1 × 48, 2 × 24, 3 × 16, 4 × 12 and 6 × 8 all make 48.
The factors of a number always include 1 and the number itself.
If a smaller number will divide exactly into a larger number, it is a factor of the larger number.
Find the factors of the numbers below and write them like the example.
The number in [brackets] is the number of factors you need to find.

1 Factors of **20** [6]
2 Factors of **18** [6]
3 Factors of **34** [4]
4 Factors of **44** [6]
5 Factors of **27** [4]

6 Factors of **49** [3]
7 Factors of **50** [6]
8 Factors of **35** [4]
9 Factors of **32** [6]
10 Factors of **60** [12]

11 Factors of **84** [12]
12 Factors of **58** [4]
13 Factors of **78** [8]
14 Factors of **80** [10]
15 Factors of **74** [4]

16 Factors of **99** [6]
17 Factors of **92** [6]
18 Factors of **100** [9]

Prime numbers only have two factors, themselves and 1.

Example   5, 7 and 11 are prime numbers because they can only be divided without a remainder by themselves and 1.

Find the one prime number from each of the sets of numbers below.

19 12, 13, 14, 15, 16
20 8, 9, 10, 11, 12
21 21, 22, 23, 24, 25, 26
22 14, 15, 16, 17, 18

23 3, 6, 8, 10, 24
24 21, 27, 33, 35, 37
25 22, 25, 31, 33, 42
26 33, 35, 43, 45

27 18, 19, 20, 21, 22
28 38, 39, 40, 41, 42
29 2, 4, 8, 16, 32
30 44, 45, 46, 47, 48, 49

Challenge

You need a partner to do this.
One of you times two minutes while the other writes down as many different prime numbers as they can.
Do not show your paper until your partner has had a go.
Compare papers and cross out any numbers that are not prime numbers.
Who managed to write down more in the two minutes?
How high is your highest prime number?

1 Kevin the supermarket shelf stacker is trying to impress his boss. He stacks
   boxes of chocolates in a triangle, in layers of 8, 7, 6, 5, 4, 3, 2 and 1.
   (a) How many boxes of chocolates does he fit in the stack?
   (b) He adds two more layers, 9 and 10 boxes. How many boxes in the
       stack now?

2 He notices the boxes at the bottom starting to be crushed.
   How many boxes will be left in the stack if he removes:
   (a) the top 3 layers
   (b) the top 5 layers
   (c) the top 6 layers?

3 Kevin has a go at making a square-based pyramid with tins of cat food.
   Each layer is a square number.
   How many tins will he need for:
   (a) 3 layers
   (b) 4 layers
   (c) 5 layers
   (d) 6 layers
   (e) 7 layers
   (f) 8 layers
   (g) 9 layers
   (h) 10 layers?

Mixed Numbers and Improper Fractions

Fractions have two parts. The lower number is the **denominator**: the number of equal parts that the whole has been divided by. The upper number is the **numerator**: the number of those equal parts that have been 'taken'.

When we combine a whole number with a fraction, we call it a **mixed number**.

Example $2\frac{1}{4}, 3\frac{1}{2}$

An **improper fraction** is a fraction whose true value is more than 1. To change mixed numbers to improper fractions, first multiply the whole number by the denominator and then add the numerator.

Example $3\frac{1}{4}$ $3 \times 4 = 12$ quarters $+ \frac{1}{4} = 13$ quarters $\frac{12}{4} + \frac{1}{4} = \frac{13}{4}$

Convert these mixed numbers into improper fractions.

1 $1\frac{3}{4} =$ 4 $4\frac{1}{3} =$ 7 $2\frac{2}{3} =$ 10 $5\frac{2}{3} =$ 13 $4\frac{9}{10} =$

2 $3\frac{1}{3} =$ 5 $2\frac{5}{8} =$ 8 $4\frac{1}{2} =$ 11 $5\frac{1}{2} =$ 14 $2\frac{3}{5} =$

3 $5\frac{1}{5} =$ 6 $1\frac{3}{10} =$ 9 $3\frac{3}{4} =$ 12 $1\frac{4}{5} =$ 15 $3\frac{3}{8} =$

To convert improper fractions into mixed numbers, divide the numerator by the denominator, which gives you the whole number part. Any remainder after dividing is the new numerator.

Example $\frac{14}{3}$ $14 \div 3 = 4$ remainder 2, so $\frac{14}{3} = 4\frac{2}{3}$

Convert these improper fractions into mixed numbers.

16 $\frac{7}{2} =$ 19 $\frac{11}{3} =$ 22 $\frac{5}{2} =$ 25 $\frac{15}{4} =$ 28 $\frac{11}{4} =$

17 $\frac{13}{6} =$ 20 $\frac{11}{2} =$ 23 $\frac{23}{6} =$ 26 $\frac{19}{5} =$ 29 $\frac{21}{8} =$

18 $\frac{27}{10} =$ 21 $\frac{9}{8} =$ 24 $\frac{16}{5} =$ 27 $\frac{17}{3} =$ 30 $\frac{37}{10} =$

Challenge

On a piece of paper, both you and a partner write down ten mixed numbers. Swap papers and see who can convert them into improper fractions first. Try the same with converting improper fractions into mixed numbers.

Comparing Fractions and Decimals

If we want to compare fractions, we need to make sure that they have the same denominator. We can change the denominator by multiplying or dividing it, **but we must do the same to the numerator** or it will alter the value of the fraction.

Example

To compare $\frac{3}{4}$ with $\frac{5}{6}$ change both into twelfths

$$\times 3 \quad\quad \frac{3}{4} = \frac{9}{12} \quad\quad \times 3$$

$$\times 2 \quad\quad \frac{5}{6} = \frac{10}{12} \quad\quad \times 2$$

Compare these pairs of fractions, changing denominators where you need to. Use <, > and =.

1 $\frac{1}{3}$ ⬤ $\frac{1}{4}$ 4 $\frac{4}{5}$ ⬤ $\frac{8}{10}$ 7 $\frac{2}{9}$ ⬤ $\frac{1}{3}$ 10 $\frac{7}{10}$ ⬤ $\frac{3}{5}$ 13 $\frac{3}{9}$ ⬤ $\frac{1}{3}$

2 $\frac{1}{2}$ ⬤ $\frac{5}{8}$ 5 $\frac{5}{12}$ ⬤ $\frac{3}{4}$ 8 $\frac{2}{7}$ ⬤ $\frac{3}{14}$ 11 $\frac{2}{3}$ ⬤ $\frac{4}{6}$ 14 $\frac{3}{7}$ ⬤ $\frac{1}{3}$

3 $\frac{5}{6}$ ⬤ $\frac{2}{3}$ 6 $\frac{3}{5}$ ⬤ $\frac{8}{15}$ 9 $\frac{1}{2}$ ⬤ $\frac{7}{8}$ 12 $\frac{1}{6}$ ⬤ $\frac{2}{12}$ 15 $\frac{1}{3}$ ⬤ $\frac{2}{5}$

If we want to compare two decimal numbers, we compare the tenths first. If the tenths numeral is the same, we then look at the hundredths to decide which is larger.

Example   0·36, 0·34   Both have 3 tenths but the second number has 4 hundredths compared to 6, so **0·36 > 0·34.**

Compare these sets of decimals using the < and > signs.

16 0·5, 0·45   18 0·78, 0·75   20 0·15, 0·4   22 0·75, 0   24 0·6, 0·66

17 0·33, 0·40   19 0·65, 0·49   21 0·09, 0·1   23 0·6, 0·55   25 0·05, 0·5

Put these in ascending order (starting with the lowest value).

26 0·4, 0·25, 0·45   28 0·09, 0·45, 0·9   30 0·3, 0·31, 0·29

27 0·22, 0·2, 0·02   29 0·51, 0·8, 0·78

Challenge

Design and make a conversion chart that will change halves, thirds, quarters and sixths into twelfths. Try making one that will convert halves, thirds, quarters, sixths, eighths and twelfths into twenty-fourths.

Fractions and Division

If we want to find a **fraction** of a number of objects, we have to divide.

Example   If we want to find $\frac{1}{5}$ of a number, we have to divide it by **5** to get the answer.

Find these fractions of these numbers.

1 $\frac{1}{2}$ of 26   3 $\frac{1}{4}$ of 36   5 $\frac{1}{10}$ of 70   7 $\frac{1}{6}$ of 54   9 $\frac{1}{4}$ of 200

2 $\frac{1}{3}$ of 39   4 $\frac{1}{3}$ of 36   6 $\frac{1}{5}$ of 45   8 $\frac{1}{3}$ of 30   10 $\frac{1}{2}$ of 720

If we want to find more than one part of a number, we start by finding one part first.

Example Find $\frac{3}{5}$ of 20. $\frac{1}{5}$ of 20 = 4 because 20 ÷ 5 = 4, so $\frac{3}{5}$ of 20 = 4 × 3 = 12.

Find these fractions of these quantities. Find one part by dividing, then more than one part by multiplying.

11 $\frac{2}{3}$ of 27   16 $\frac{3}{5}$ of 55   21 $\frac{2}{3}$ of 153   26 $\frac{3}{5}$ of 85

12 $\frac{3}{4}$ of 36   17 $\frac{7}{8}$ of 48   22 $\frac{3}{10}$ of 760   27 $\frac{3}{8}$ of 88

13 $\frac{2}{3}$ of 42   18 $\frac{3}{4}$ of 240   23 $\frac{4}{5}$ of 120   28 $\frac{7}{8}$ of 104

14 $\frac{5}{6}$ of 42   19 $\frac{3}{8}$ of 320   24 $\frac{3}{8}$ of 160   29 $\frac{5}{6}$ of 126

15 $\frac{2}{3}$ of 66   20 $\frac{5}{6}$ of 78   25 $\frac{7}{10}$ of 350   30 $\frac{9}{10}$ of 140

Challenge

On squared paper, draw a rectangle 18 squares wide and 20 squares deep.
Colour one quarter yellow, two tenths blue, three eighths green and one sixth red.
Colour the remaining squares black.
How many squares of each colour do you have?
Do another rectangle and choose what fractions of the rectangle are going to be what colour.

Decimals

Some numbers have digits with a value of less than 1 unit. We use a **decimal point** to separate them from the whole numbers. To the left of the decimal point are whole numbers. To the right of the decimal point are digits worth less than 1 unit.

H	T	U	$\frac{1}{10}$	$\frac{1}{100}$
		3 ·	2	5
		0 ·	5	5

When you work with decimal numbers, make sure you write them down with the decimal points in line. You only **need** to write in zeros that are between digits, or between a digit and the decimal point.

Write down the value of the digit that is in **bold print**.

Example 1·3**7**   The 3 is worth **3 tenths**.
3·3**4**   The 4 is worth **4 hundredths**.

1 5·6**5**
2 4·0**6**
3 0·1**2**
4 2**6**·34
5 1**2**5·98
6 50·2**4**
7 40·2**7**
8 534·5**7**
9 102·0**8**
10 82·**5**0
11 35·**0**6
12 4**7**·81
13 240·**9**5
14 123·4**5**
15 98**7**·63

Write these numbers down in ascending order (starting with the lowest).

16 15·55, 15·5, 15·2
17 1·5, 1·08, 1·6
18 15·4, 0·80, 0·75
19 5·6, 5·5, 5·09
20 20·8, 20·25, 20·99
21 12·25, 11·5, 10·75
22 9·9, 10·10, 10·01
23 4·5, 0·45, 45
24 0·6, 40, 0·59

Write these numbers down in descending order (starting with the highest).

25 50·5, 0·51, 5·05
26 10·8, 18·0, 10·08
27 25·0, 20·5, 2·50
28 0·34, 3·40, 34·04
29 7·65, 7·76, 76·56
30 0·05, 1·92, 0·85

Challenge

Draw a long line and label the start of it **0**, and the end of it **100**. Mark **50** in the middle.
Estimate and mark on the line where you would place the numbers used in questions 25 to 30.

Rounding Decimals

Sometimes we don't need to include the hundredths in a number. Instead, we round the decimal part up or down to the **nearest whole number**. If the decimal part is **less than 0·50**, we round **down** by missing it out. If the decimal part is **0·50 or more**, we round **up** by adding 1 to the units.

Example   24·35 rounds down to **24**   32·51 rounds up to **33**
Round these numbers to the nearest whole number.

1 1·90	5 120·66	9 55·75	13 1528·52
2 21·09	6 9·11	10 168·45	14 2560·40
3 7·50	7 521·65	11 249·81	15 624·5
4 33·33	8 54·25	12 950·36	

Sometimes we need to be a little more accurate and round up or down to the **nearest tenth**. If the hundredth digit is **less than 5** we round **down** by missing it out. If the hundredth digit is 5 or more, we round **up** by adding a tenth. If there is already a 9 in the tenths column, you will have to round up to the next whole number.

Example
63·34 rounds down to **63·3**   42·55 rounds up to **42·6**   27·96 rounds up to **28·0**
Round these numbers to the nearest tenth.

16 36·36	20 4·66	24 65·59	28 3658·37
17 21·15	21 18·94	25 128·44	29 32·83
18 32·82	22 120·78	26 47·96	30 69·99
19 72·51	23 96·31	27 1505·52	

Challenge

Measure the length of a number of items that are longer than half a metre.
Round the lengths to:
(a) the nearest tenth of a metre
(b) the nearest whole metre.

Multiplying and Dividing Decimals by 10 and 100

When we write numbers with more than one digit, the position of each digit tells us its value. Each column is ten times the value of the column to its right, and one tenth of the value of the column to its left.
We can use this fact to multiply by 10 or 100, simply moving the digits one or two columns **to the left**. To multiply 3·25 by 10 move them one column. To multiply 3·25 by 100 move them two columns.
You only need to write in zeros that are between digits, or between a digit and the decimal point.
Complete these equations by moving the digits one or two columns to the left.

```
          |  |
H T U    10 100
      3 · 2  5
    3 2 · 5  0
  3 2 5 · 0  0
```

1 10·45 × 10 =

2 3·33 × 100 =

3 15·78 × 10 =

4 13·52 × 100 =

5 190·66 × 10 =

6 25·75 × 100 =

7 40·16 × 100 =

8 3·33 × 100 =

9 180·25 × 10 =

10 324·75 × 10 =

11 45·25 × 100 =

12 92·5 × 100 =

13 38·08 × 100 =

14 99·46 × 10 =

15 108·06 × 10 =

To divide by 10 or 100, simply move the digits one or two columns **to the right**.

16 50·4 ÷ 10 =

17 125 ÷ 100 =

18 320·8 ÷ 10 =

19 12·5 ÷ 100 =

20 527·8 ÷ 10 =

21 58·5 ÷ 100 =

22 650 ÷ 100 =

23 623·25 ÷ 10 =

24 42·6 ÷ 100 =

25 750·75 ÷ 10 =

26 15 ÷ 100 =

27 0·46 ÷ 10 =

28 9·9 ÷ 100 =

29 0·01 ÷ 10 =

30 7 ÷ 100 =

Challenge

When we are working in rough, it can be easier to move the decimal point the opposite way instead of moving the digits.
Copy this movable decimal point onto card, then use it to multiply and divide by 10 and 100.
You will need to space your digits out when you write them down.

```
Th H T U    1/10  1/100  1/1000
```

Fractions, Decimals and Percentages

When we use fractions that are hundredths, we can write them as decimals.

Example $\frac{75}{100} = 0.75$ $\frac{5}{100} = 0.05$ $\frac{10}{100} = 0.10$

1 $\frac{25}{100} =$ 2 $\frac{33}{100} =$ 3 $\frac{67}{100} =$ 4 $\frac{8}{100} =$ 5 $\frac{20}{100} =$

Change these decimals into fractions.

6 0.40   7 0.11   8 0.45   9 0.95   10 0.5

We can use percentages instead of hundredths of decimals. **Per cent** means 'for each hundred'. The sign for per cent is %. For example, 75 hundredths is 75 per cent.
Change these fractions into percentages.

11 $\frac{34}{100} =$ % 12 $\frac{18}{100} =$ % 13 $\frac{45}{100} =$ % 14 $\frac{76}{100} =$ % 15 $\frac{50}{100} =$ %

Change these decimals into percentages.

16 0.30 = % 17 0.74 = % 18 0.22 = % 19 0.85 = % 20 0.5 = %

Change these percentages into fractions.

21 27% = $\frac{}{100}$ 22 50% = $\frac{}{100}$ 23 33% = $\frac{}{100}$ 24 25% = $\frac{}{100}$ 25 70% = $\frac{}{100}$

Change these percentages into decimals.

26 5% =   27 75% =   28 60% =   29 85% =   30 3% =

Challenge

Change $\frac{1}{10}, \frac{2}{10}, \frac{3}{10}, \frac{4}{10}, \frac{5}{10}, \frac{6}{10}, \frac{7}{10}, \frac{8}{10}$ and $\frac{9}{10}$ into percentages.
How would you change thousandths into percentages?

Percentages of Whole Numbers

Remember that 1% means the same as $\frac{1}{100}$.

50% is the same as $\frac{1}{2}$, 25% is the same as $\frac{1}{4}$ and 75% is the same as $\frac{3}{4}$.

10% is the same as $\frac{1}{10}$, so 20% is the same as $\frac{2}{10}$.

An easy way to find 30%, 40%, 60%, and so on, is first to find 10%, then multiply by 3, 4, 6, etc.

An easy way to find 5% is first to find 10%, then halve it.

Find the following.

1   10% of 80

2   25% of 96

3   20% of 80

4   50% of 400

5   75% of 400

6   60% of 30

7   5% of 300

8   80% of 70

9   50% of 520

10 25% of £480

11 70% of £900

12 75% of £900

13 15% of £200

14 90% of £120

15 50% of £3524

Sometimes the only way to find a percentage of a number is to divide it by 100 to find 1%, then multiply it by the percentage required.

Example   7% of £800   1% of £800 is £8 so 7% is 7 × £8 = **£56**

You might need decimals to divide by 100. See Unit 17 for how to do it.

Try using this method to find the following.

16 6% of 300

17 17% of 400

18 5% of 2000

19 2% of 500

20 6% of 300p

21 8% of 200p

22 15% of £200

23 4% of £4·00

24 7% of £5

25 9% of £3

26 7% of £10

27 12% of £6

28 3% of £20

29 16% of £8

30 51% of £20

Challenge

Make up some easier ways to find these percentages of a number: 15%, 45%, 90%, 95% and 99%.

Try out your 'easy way'.

15 + 85 = 100, so 15% of a number + 85% of the same number must equal the whole number. See if you can use this to find a way of checking some of your answers.

Fractions, Decimals and Percentages of Money and Measures

On this page you are asked to find parts of amounts of
money and parts of measures.
If you have forgotten how to find a fraction, look back
at Unit 18.
If you have forgotten how to divide by 10 or 20 to find a decimal,
look back at Unit 17.
If you have forgotten how to find a percentage, look back at Unit 19.
Tip   It might be easier if you change to smaller units: £ to p, m to cm and so on.
Find:

1 $\frac{2}{3}$ of £18 =

2 $\frac{3}{5}$ of £150 =

3 $\frac{7}{8}$ of £32 =

4 $\frac{5}{6}$ of £3·60 =

5 $\frac{3}{4}$ of £2 =

6 $\frac{9}{10}$ of £2·20 =

7 $\frac{3}{4}$ of 320 cm =

8 $\frac{3}{5}$ of 650 cm =

9 $\frac{3}{7}$ of 287 cm =

10 $\frac{3}{8}$ of 3·2 m =

11 $\frac{4}{5}$ of 4 m =

12 $\frac{5}{8}$ of 4 m =

13 $\frac{3}{5}$ of 500 g =

14 $\frac{4}{9}$ of 450 g =

15 $\frac{7}{10}$ of 3 kg =

16 50% of 5 kg =

17 20% of 4 kg =

18 75% of 6 kg =

19 10% of 2 m =

20 25% of 8 m =

21 3% of 2 m =

22 20% of £3 =

23 75% of £6 =

24 7% of £5 =

25 0·25 m =   cm

26 0·6 m =   cm

27 0·33 m =   cm

28 1·5 m =   cm

29 2·3 m =   cm

30 10·8 m =   cm

Challenge

Using fractions and decimals, and different units (for example, kg and g), see how
many ways you can record **35 grams**.
Try doing the same with **8 metres**. (You could change it into km, cm and mm.)

1 Tanya tried a job as a trainee surveyor.
   She had to measure lengths and areas.
   She was left on her own and got her
   measurements muddled up.
   (a) Sort out her measures into a set of
       length measurements and area
       measurements.
   (b) Change all the length measurements
       into the same format and then put
       them into ascending order (starting
       with the shortest length).
   (c) Change all the area measurements
       into the same format and then put
       them into ascending order (starting
       with the smallest area).
       Reminder 1 m^2 (square metre)
       = 10 000 cm^2 (square centimetres)

| R.O.W |
| Land Surveys Limited |

180 cm   7240 mm

2.4 m^2

643.5 cm   5.8 m

5678 cm

10 825 cm^2

210 cm^2 0.25 km   0.2 m^2

2.5 m

976 mm   951 m^2

4325 cm^2

2 Her next job was selling building
   materials, but she still got confused.
   (a) Sort out her measures into a set
       of lengths and a set of weights.
   (b) Put the lengths in order, starting
       with the shortest length.
   (c) Put the weights in order, starting
       with the heaviest.

BODGIT
Builder's Supplies

3 tonnes
                560 kg
       2525 cm
                3 kg
70 m   500 g
        0.75 kg
0.5 tonnes   365 cm
                    8.5 m
            9.99 m
7350 mm   77 mm
        5000 kg
99.9 cm   600 g

Addition and Subtraction

Complete these equations.

1 35 + ⬭ = 100

2 100 − 34 = ⬭

3 33 + 12 + ⬭ = 100

4 100 − 58 = ⬭

5 48 + ⬭ = 100

6 100 − 71 = ⬭

7 49 + 15 + ⬭ = 100

8 27 + 13 + ⬭ = 100

9 67 + ⬭ = 100

10 26 + ⬭ = 100

11 100 − 63 = ⬭

12 42 + ⬭ = 100

13 24 + 36 + ⬭ = 100

14 72 + ⬭ = 100

15 34 + 42 + ⬭ = 100

Complete these equations using decimal numbers.

16 0·22 + 0·74 = ⬭

17 0·75 − 0·25 = ⬭

18 0·65 + 0·35 = ⬭

19 0·45 + 0·⬭ = 1

20 0·82 + 0·⬭ = 1

21 0·25 + 0·⬭ = 1

22 1 − 0·55 = ⬭

23 0·32 + 0·35 + 0·⬭ = 1

24 1 − 0·82 = ⬭

25 0·45 + 0·15 + 0·⬭ = 1

26 0·25 + 0·20 + 0·⬭ = 1

27 1 − 0·05 = ⬭

28 0·14 + 0·25 + 0·23 = ⬭

29 0·62 + 0·05 + 0·13 = ⬭

30 0·08 + 0·08 + 0·16 = ⬭

Challenge

Use a calculator to make 20 pairs of decimal numbers that add up to 1.

Adding Using Partitioning

An easy way of adding two three-digit numbers
is to partition it into hundreds, tens and units.

Example   235 + 421
200 + 400 = **600**, 30 + 20 = **50**, 5 + 1 = **6**, so 600 + 50 + 6 = **656**
Use this method to complete these equations.

1 426 + 343 =

2 425 + 264 =

3 504 + 393 =

4 617 + 252 =

5 425 + 463 =

6 519 + 320 =

Sometimes we need to exchange from units to tens, and from tens to hundreds.

Example   463 + 278
400 + 200 = **600**, 60 + 70 = **130**, 3 + 8 = **11**, so 600 + 130 + 11 = **744**

7 628 + 278 =

8 466 + 227 =

9 395 + 564 =

10 246 + 338 =

11 434 + 475 =

12 156 + 387 =

13 735 + 182 =

14 538 + 209 =

15 428 + 473 =

You can use the same partitioning method to add up numbers that include decimals.

Example   4·3 + 3·6 = 7 + 0·9 = **7·9**
You may need to exchange.

16 3·3 + 3·6 =

17 6·2 + 4·2 =

18 2·4 + 7·3 =

19 7·1 + 6·8 =

20 6·8 + 4·1 =

21 6·5 + 7·4 =

22 3·7 + 6·5 =

23 6·3 + 2·9 =

24 5·8 + 4·2 =

25 1·5 + 7·8 =

26 8·8 + 0·9 =

27 6·2 + 2·8 =

28 6·4 + 5·9 =

29 7·7 + 3·3 =

30 8·7 + 7·8 =

Challenge

Can you add three three-digit numbers using the partitioning method?
Make up five addition equations and swap them with a partner.
See who is the first to complete all ten **correctly**.
Repeat with three decimal numbers like the ones used in questions 16 to 30.
With a partner make up five each, swap them, and see who completes them
correctly first.

Near Doubles

You should already know some double numbers without having to work them out. You can use this knowledge to add **near doubles** in your head.

Example   36 + 38 is close to double 36 or double 38.
Either double 36 and add 2 on, or double 38 and take 2 off.
(36 × 2) + 2 = 72 + 2 = 74   (38 × 2) − 2 = 76 − 2 = 74
If there is a difference of 2 between the numbers, you can double the number that comes between. 37 × 2 = 74

Do these equations in your head.

1 66 + 67 =   3 73 + 72 =   5 95 + 94 =

2 57 + 56 =   4 85 + 86 =   6 65 + 66 =

The following equations are easy if you think of them as a number of tens.

Example   230 + 240 is 23 tens + 24 tens.
Double 24 to 48 and take 1 off = 47 tens = 470.

7 260 + 270 =   9 360 + 370 =   11 650 + 640 =

8 450 + 440 =   10 500 + 510 =   12 390 + 400 =

Work these out in your head.

13 406 + 407 =   16 152 + 150 =   19 748 + 750 =

14 325 + 327 =   17 279 + 281 =   20 379 + 380 =

15 290 + 288 =   18 227 + 229 =   21 524 + 526 =

You can use 'near doubles' to add up decimal numbers.

22 22·5 + 22·4 =   25 0·38 + 0·40 =   28 12·25 + 12·23 =

23 15·5 + 14·5 =   26 33·33 + 33·34 =   29 0·48 + 0·5 =

24 1·8 + 1·7 =   27 5·4 + 5·3 =   30 19·5 + 20 =

Challenge

Choose some three-digit whole numbers and split them into pairs of near doubles.

Example   351 = 175 + 176   483 = 242 + 241

Near Multiples

When you have to add or subtract 8 or 9 units in your head, you can 'cheat' by adding or subtracting 10 or a multiple of 10 (20, 30, 40, etc.) then correcting the error.

Example

47 + 18 =	Add **20** instead of 18.	47 + **20** = 67
	You've added 2 too many, so take 2 away.	67 − 2 = 65
86 − 29	Subtract **30** instead 29.	86 − **30** = 56
	You've taken away 1 too many, so add 1 more.	56 + 1 = 57

This is called using **near multiples** of 10.
Use this method to complete the equations below, in your head.

1 58 + 26 =   4 90 − 41 =   7 117 − 29 =   10 94 + 89 =

2 84 − 48 =   5 74 + 19 =   8 83 + 58 =   11 265 − 78 =

3 63 + 39 =   6 144 + 38 =   9 133 − 38 =   12 246 + 59 =

You can use this short-cut to add or subtract 'near multiples' of 100.

Example   474 + 198 =   Add **200** instead of 198.   474 + **200** = 674
You've added 2 too many, so take 2 away.   674 − 2 = 672

---

13 356 + 297 =   16 951 − 794 =   19 728 + 180 =   22 456 + 195 =

14 451 − 203 =   17 545 + 190 =   20 563 − 192 =   23 864 − 395 =

15 542 − 398 =   18 353 + 198 =   21 434 − 188 =   24 848 + 498 =

You can use 'near multiples' of 1 unit when you are adding or subtracting decimals.

Example   32·7 + 1·8 =   Add **2** instead of 1·8.   32·7 + **2** = 34·7
Take off the extra 0·2 that you added.   34·7 − 0·2 = 34·5
Use this method to work out these equations in your head.

25 23·5 + 24·9 =   27 57·6 + 2·1 =   29 63·8 + 25·9 =

26 45·6 − 14·9 =   28 12·0 − 3·1 =   30 45·6 − 11·8 =

Challenge

Find other ways of using 'near multiples' to make addition and subtraction easier: for example, working with thousands.
Can you use 'near multiples' to add measures such as 4·39 m?

Tricks for Adding in Your Head

Look for any pairs of numbers that make 10 and add them first.

Example $7 + 5 + 3 + 6$ Add 7 and 3 to make 10, then add on the 5 and 6.

Look for any doubles (e.g. $6 + 6$) and near doubles (e.g. $7 + 8$).

Example $4 + 8 + 5 + 8$ Double the 8 (16), add the 4 (20), then add the 5.

Look for numbers to take your total to the next multiple of 10.

Example $7 + 5 + 6 + 8$ Add 7 and 8 (15), add 5 (20), then add the 6.

Find pairs of numbers that make the same as another number.

Example $9 + 3 + 5 + 2$ Add 2 and 3 (5), double (10), then add the 9.

Split numbers up to take the total to the next multiple of 10.

Example $17 + 7$ Add 3 of the 7 to 17 (20), then add the 4.

Add these sets of numbers up in your head. Choose which tricks you want to use.

1 $8 + 5 + 2 + 4 =$

2 $6 + 5 + 4 + 6 =$

3 $7 + 5 + 7 + 2 =$

4 $7 + 5 + 2 + 9 =$

5 $4 + 6 + 9 + 5 =$

6 $3 + 3 + 8 + 4 =$

7 $5 + 9 + 8 + 7 =$

8 $9 + 6 + 5 + 1 =$

9 $7 + 6 + 8 + 1 =$

10 $5 + 7 + 15 =$

11 $12 + 5 + 8 =$

12 $7 + 15 + 23 =$

13 $3 + 14 + 5 + 6 =$

14 $21 + 8 + 19 + 8 =$

15 $13 + 8 + 2 + 5 =$

16 $16 + 8 + 9 + 2 =$

17 $6 + 7 + 24 + 8 =$

18 $22 + 3 + 8 + 5 =$

19 $9 + 7 + 11 + 5 =$

20 $28 + 7 + 2 + 7 =$

21 $17 + 5 + 7 + 2 =$

When you use these with decimals, be careful with the decimal point.

22 $0.3 + 0.9 + 0.7 =$

23 $0.8 + 0.8 + 0.2 =$

24 $1.4 + 0.7 + 0.6 =$

25 $0.5 + 0.7 + 0.2 + 1.5 =$

26 $2.7 + 0.7 + 0.6 + 1.4 =$

27 $0.9 + 0.6 + 1.1 + 0.4 =$

28 $0.7 + 0.6 + 0.5 + 2.3 =$

29 $0.4 + 0.7 + 0.5 + 7.6 =$

30 $1.4 + 1.5 + 0.3 + 1.6 =$

Challenge

Look at some of the equations on this page.

Write down the order you added them up in, to show the tricks you used.

Try adding them up in a different order – are there other tricks you could have used?

Adding and Subtracting with HTU 1

When you add or subtract in your head, it can be easier to treat the tens and units separately.

Example $45 + 31 = (40 + 30) + (5 + 1)$.
4 tens + 3 tens = 7 tens (**70**) then add on the 5 + 1 (**6**) = 76
$45 - 31 = (40 - 30) + (5 - 1)$.
4 tens − 3 tens = 1 ten (**10**) then add on the 5 − 1 (**4**) = 14

Work these out in your head.

1 $145 + 23 =$ 5 $341 + 38 =$ 9 $752 + 44 =$ 13 $374 + 24 =$

2 $86 - 43 =$ 6 $549 - 36 =$ 10 $365 - 32 =$ 14 $568 - 47 =$

3 $236 + 42 =$ 7 $262 + 22 =$ 11 $335 + 42 =$ 15 $246 + 53 =$

4 $245 - 43 =$ 8 $648 - 31 =$ 12 $455 - 34 =$

Sometimes you will need to exchange like this:

Example $45 + 37 = (40 + 30) + (5 + 7)$.
Add up the **70 + 10 + 2 = 82**
$735 - 374 = (700 - 300) + (30 - 70) + (5 - 4)$.
You can't take 7 tens from 3 tens so treat it like this: **(600 − 300) +
(13 tens− 7 tens) + (5 − 4)**.
300 + 60 + 1 = 361

Work these out in your head.

16 $247 + 34 =$ 21 $284 - 45 =$ 26 $473 + 52 =$

17 $174 - 47 =$ 22 $194 + 17 =$ 27 $363 - 92 =$

18 $136 + 44 =$ 23 $242 - 18 =$ 28 $386 + 46 =$

19 $363 - 26 =$ 24 $561 - 35 =$ 29 $523 + 88 =$

20 $444 + 83 =$ 25 $173 - 66 =$ 30 $456 + 97 =$

Challenge

Look through the equations again and look for other short-cuts you could have used to find the correct answer. You might look for these short-cuts:

- near doubles (see Unit 24)
- near multiples (see Unit 25).

Adding and Subtracting with HTU 2

When you add or subtract in your head, it can be
easier to treat the hundreds, tens and units separately.

Example   423 + 341 = (400 + 300) + (20 + 40) + (3 + 1).
700 + 60 + 4 = 764

673 − 241 = (600 − 200) + (70 − 40) + (3 − 1).
400 + 30 + 2 = 432

Work these out in your head.

1 735 + 144 =   5 474 + 213 =   9 274 + 413 =   13 425 + 474 =
2 575 − 542 =   6 599 − 297 =   10 615 − 512 =   14 478 − 370 =
3 412 + 427 =   7 564 + 237=   11 743 + 155 =   15 516 + 415 =
4 658 − 416 =   8 584 − 404 =   12 387 − 367 =

Sometimes you will need to exchange like this:
Example   565 + 372 = (500 + 300) + (30 + 70) + (5 + 2).
800 + 100 + 30 + 7 = 937
Example   75 − 37 = (70 − 30) + (5 − 7) = (60 − 30) + (15 − 7)
30 + 8 = 38

Work these out in your head.

16 636 + 182 =   20 478 + 326 =   24 632 − 315 =   28 637 + 274 =
17 584 − 146 =   21 808 − 451 =   25 835 − 428 =   29 137 + 376 =
18 456 + 462 =   22 816 + 148 =   26 451 + 499 =   30 526 + 293 =
19 615 − 262 =   23 729 − 231 =   27 913 − 614 =

Challenge

You need to work with a partner, but don't let your partner see what you are doing!
On paper each write down five equations like the ones above and work out the
answers.
Each make a copy without the answers.
Time how long it takes your partner to work out the answers correctly **in their head**.
Time how long it takes you to work out theirs.
Were the two sets of five equations equally difficult?
Agree some rules and try again − see who is faster.

Problems 4

1 A local ice-cream parlour has introduced
   some new products and is keeping a
   check on the sales.

	Monday	Tuesday	Wednesday	Thursday	Friday	Saturday
grape-flavoured lolly	548	685	541	542	681	968
tomato-flavoured lolly	6	18	13	25	19	27

(a) Which days have the least sales?
(b) Which day has the most sales?
(c) What is the difference between the best sales day and the worst?
(d) What is the difference between the best sales day and the worst for
     each flavour?

2 As part of a road safety project, the council is counting traffic passing a school.
   It counts the vehicles passing for 1 hour before and after school.

Morning	Monday	Tuesday	Wednesday	Thursday	Friday
cars and small vans	745	634	368	487	586
large vans and lorries	254	176	284	165	134
Afternoon					
cars and small vans	557	495	378	269	251
large vans and lorries	356	312	188	205	85

(a) Which day is busiest for cars and small vans?
(b) Which day is quietest for cars and small vans?
(c) Which day is busiest for large vans and lorries?
(d) Which day is quietest for large vans and lorries?
(e) Which day has the busiest morning traffic?
(f) Which day has the busiest afternoon traffic?
(g) Which day has the quietest morning traffic?
(h) Which day has the quietest afternoon traffic?

Adding and Subtracting on Paper

Copy and work out these additions in columns. **If** you need to exchange, remember to show it below the line.

Example

```
  46849
+  5536
───────
  52385
  I I I I
```

1
```
  2433
+ 3342
```

4
```
  7725
+ 2057
```

7
```
  49905
+   349
```

10
```
  52873
+   687
```

13
```
  80587
+  1604
```

2
```
  4293
+ I576
```

5
```
  6037
+ 2540
```

8
```
  66446
+  3443
```

11
```
  65773
+ 25735
```

14
```
  29645
+ 40832
```

3
```
  5838
+ 2541
```

6
```
  26584
+  3975
```

9
```
  67433
+  2594
```

12
```
  7865
+ 3486
```

15
```
  36858
+ 38541
```

Copy and work out these subtractions. **If** you have to exchange a ten from the tens to the units or a hundred from the hundreds to the tens, remember to show the exchanging at the top.

Example

```
  6 3²Ⅎ⁵
-   2118
────────
  4217
```

16
```
  6673
-  539
```

19
```
  26945
-  3847
```

22
```
  65775
- 42017
```

25
```
  83663
- 34656
```

28
```
  75104
- 12856
```

17
```
  7685
- 3445
```

20
```
  36258
-  3491
```

23
```
  48376
- 35121
```

26
```
  56067
- 46734
```

29
```
  60858
- 36249
```

18
```
  8057
- 6304
```

21
```
  47630
- 30514
```

24
```
  71542
- 21359
```

27
```
  64738
- 32767
```

30
```
  97634
- 59665
```

Challenge

Check the subtractions by adding the number you took away to the answer.

Adding on Paper

2156+3456+9374+∑

Copy and work out these additions in columns. **If** you need to exchange units for tens, tens for hundreds or hundreds for thousands, show it below the line.

```
  57223
   2349
+  4356
───────
  63928
 ı  ı ı
```

1
```
   2351
   1296
+   118
───────
```

2
```
  35572
   1543
+   264
───────
```

3
```
  25047
   8313
+   324
───────
```

4
```
  27350
   3645
+   457
───────
```

5
```
  24616
   4029
+   628
───────
```

6
```
  34554
  42547
+  2864
───────
```

7
```
  90909
  81481
+  7474
───────
```

8
```
  64028
  26338
+  6423
───────
```

9
```
  84123
  40956
+  3721
───────
```

10
```
  53275
  58340
+  8778
───────
```

11
```
  47943
  65783
+ 43689
───────
```

12
```
  64538
  28267
+ 18965
───────
```

13
```
  19822
  71230
+ 13571
───────
```

14
```
  35632
  37535
+ 20365
───────
```

15
```
  27950
  49389
+ 23541
───────
```

16
```
  35053
  31427
+ 30759
───────
```

17
```
  13833
  45463
+ 28670
───────
```

18
```
  15148
  26390
+ 58246
───────
```

19
```
  47438
  16354
+ 28485
───────
```

20
```
  43587
  22534
+ 26867
───────
```

21
```
   1423
   2163
    321
+   501
───────
```

22
```
   2324
   3524
   3835
+   279
───────
```

23
```
   3654
   3669
   1517
+  2547
───────
```

24
```
  35687
  22625
   3352
+  2784
───────
```

25
```
  42285
  31065
  15908
+ 31554
───────
```

Challenge

Make up some large additions of your own by using people's telephone numbers. If you wish, you could miss out one of the digits, and perhaps miss out the area code.

Adding and Subtracting Decimals on Paper

Copy and work out these additions in columns. Put the decimal point in the answer row **before you start to add**. Show any exchanging below the line in the usual way.

Example

```
  34·66
+ 26·75
------
  61·41
  | |  |
```

1.
```
  25·66
+ 24·23
------
```

4.
```
  33·46
+ 63·39
------
```

7.
```
  315·83
+  22·67
------
```

10.
```
  375·74
+  54·98
------
```

13.
```
  378·58
+ 341·69
------
```

2.
```
  48·46
+ 26·94
------
```

5.
```
  27·74
+ 53·06
------
```

8.
```
  653·26
+  75·19
------
```

11.
```
  822·50
+ 343·54
------
```

14.
```
  789·99
+ 124·99
------
```

3.
```
  84·57
+ 16·55
------
```

6.
```
  336·96
+  45·18
------
```

9.
```
  307·85
+  43·57
------
```

12.
```
  164·75
+ 763·56
------
```

15.
```
  466·67
+ 742·24
------
```

Copy and work out these subtractions in columns. Put the decimal point in the answer row **before you start to subtract**. Show any exchanging above the line in the usual way.

```
     2 1
  63·3⁵5
-  21·18
------
  42·17
```

16.
```
  66·98
- 43·55
------
```

19.
```
  543·54
-  49·75
------
```

22.
```
  766·05
- 534·75
------
```

25.
```
  404·63
- 219·49
------
```

28.
```
  7453·60
-  617·43
------
```

17.
```
  286·83
-  23·27
------
```

20.
```
  765·28
-  86·51
------
```

23.
```
  416·60
- 114·75
------
```

26.
```
  6422·86
-  367·49
------
```

29.
```
  8564·53
- 4682·34
------
```

18.
```
  246·54
-  28·45
------
```

21.
```
  976·43
- 453·54
------
```

24.
```
  636·02
- 621·89
------
```

27.
```
  4805·45
-  374·64
------
```

30.
```
  8563·06
- 6548·33
------
```

Challenge

Check the subtractions by adding the number you took away to the answer.

Problems 5

The headteacher has spent too long on paperwork and has finally gone completely mad. Here are just two of the symptoms.

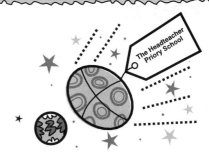

The Headteacher
Priory School

1 He has decided to count the furniture, 'just in case a meteor lands on the school'.
   (a) Use his notebook and add up his totals for each item.
   (b) Total up how many chairs, tables and cupboards each class has.

	'infant' tables	'junior' tables	'infant' chairs	'junior' chairs	'adult' chairs	small cupboards	large cupboards	sets of bookshelves
Nursery	12		18		2	8	4	5
Reception	18		32		3	6	2	3
Class 1	20		35		1	7	1	6
Class 2	12	8	20	7	2	5	3	4
Class 3	4	11	8	26	1	5	2	2
Class 4	2	14	1	32	3	4	1	3
Class 5		18		17	14	6	2	2
Class 6		17		8	25	6	3	2

2 He spent last Friday hiding in the stockroom instead of going to a headteachers' meeting. While in there he did more counting!
   (a) Add up his totals.
   (b) Add up the ballpoint pens.
   (c) Add up the fine felt pens.
   (d) Add up the red pens.
   (e) Add up the blue pens.
   (f) Add up the black pens.
   (g) Add up the children's scissors.
   (h) Add up the adults' scissors.

pencil crayons		scissors		folders		pens	
black	37	**adults**		blue	5	ballpoint red	49
blue	34	good quality	2	cream	187	ballpoint blue	63
green	157	poor quality	13	green	25	ballpoint black	24
orange	83	bent and broken	5	grey	153	ballpoint green	165
purple	53	**children's**		orange	37	fine felt black	37
red	38	left-handed	48	red	29	fine felt blue	86
yellow	72	right-handed	27	yellow	14	fine felt red	57

Multiplication and Division 1

Multiplication and division are **inverse operations** – they do the opposite of each other.

We can 'undo' a multiplication by dividing the answer like this: $6 \times 7 = 42, 42 \div 7 = 6$

We can 'undo' a division by multiplying the answer like this: $16 \div 2 = 8, 8 \times 2 = 16$

Complete these equations and then check by 'undoing' what you have done.

Example $5 \times 6 = 30$, so undo it by dividing: $30 \div 6 = 5$

$48 \div 8 = 6$, so undo it by multiplying: $6 \times 8 = 48$

1 $36 \div 6 = \quad , \quad \times 6 = \quad$ 7 $32 \div 4 = \quad , \quad \times 4 = \quad$ 13 $42 \div 7 = \quad , \quad \times 7 = \quad$

2 $3 \times 7 = \quad , \quad \div 7 = \quad$ 8 $4 \times 9 = \quad , \quad \div 9 = \quad$ 14 $8 \times 8 = \quad , \quad \div 8 = \quad$

3 $56 \div 8 = \quad , \quad \times 8 = \quad$ 9 $36 \div 9 = \quad , \quad \times 9 = \quad$ 15 $28 \div 4 = \quad , \quad \times 4 = \quad$

4 $8 \times 4 = \quad , \quad \div 4 = \quad$ 10 $8 \times 3 = \quad , \quad \div 3 = \quad$ 16 $7 \times 10 = \quad , \quad \div 10 = \quad$

5 $49 \div 7 = \quad , \quad \times 7 = \quad$ 11 $63 \div 7 = \quad , \quad \times 7 = \quad$ 17 $72 \div 8 = \quad , \quad \times 8 = \quad$

6 $7 \times 6 = \quad , \quad \div 6 = \quad$ 12 $5 \times 8 = \quad , \quad \div 8 = \quad$ 18 $6 \times 9 = \quad , \quad \div 9 = \quad$

We can use brackets to show the separate parts of the calculation. Work out the part(s) in brackets first.

Example $(3 \times 6) + (6 \times 7) = 18 + 42 = 60$

If there are brackets inside other brackets, work from the inside first.

Example $(2 \times (14 - 2)) \div (3 \times (18 \div 9))$

$14 - 2$ is 12 and $18 \div 9$ is 2, so: $(2 \times 12) \div (3 \times 2) \rightarrow 24 \div 6 = 4$

19 $(8 \times 4) + (5 \times 6) =$ 25 $4 \times (6 + 3) =$

20 $(6 \times 6) \div (20 \div 5) =$ 26 $6 \times (42 \div 7) =$

21 $(12 + 28) \div (32 \div 4) =$ 27 $4 \times (43 - 36) =$

22 $(56 \div 7) \times (43 - 36) =$ 28 $(3 \times (18 - 13)) + (4 (3 + 5)) =$

23 $(36 \div 4) \times (48 \div 6) =$ 29 $(4 \times (4 + 5)) - (3 \times (17 - 9)) =$

24 $(8 \times 5) - (6 \times 4) =$ 30 $(8 \times (45 \div 9)) \div (2 \times (12 - 7)) =$

Challenge

Make up five bracket equations and swap them with five that a partner has done. See who finishes first!

Quotients and Remainders

When we divide one number by another, the answer is called the **quotient**. If the number does not divide exactly into the other, the quotient may include a fraction.

Example $9 \div 2 = 4\frac{1}{2}$ $15 \div 4 = 3\frac{3}{4}$ $29 \div 9 = 3\frac{2}{9}$

In the fraction part of the quotient, the **numerator** (upper numeral) is the remainder, and the **denominator** (the lower numeral) is the number we divided by. Complete these division equations, writing in the remainder as a fraction.

1 $38 \div 3 =$ 3 $46 \div 5 =$ 5 $53 \div 9 =$ 7 $95 \div 9 =$ 9 $25 \div 3 =$

2 $67 \div 8 =$ 4 $39 \div 7 =$ 6 $41 \div 6 =$ 8 $39 \div 4 =$

When we divide by 2, 4, 5 or 10, we can also give the quotient as a decimal number because a quarter = 0·25, a half = 0·50, a tenth = 0·1, and a fifth = 0·2.

Example $15 \div 4 = 3\frac{3}{4} = 3·75$

10 $19 \div 2 =$ 13 $89 \div 10 =$ 16 $52 \div 5 =$

11 $34 \div 5 =$ 14 $41 \div 4 =$ 17 $63 \div 10 =$

12 $27 \div 4 =$ 15 $31 \div 2 =$

Sometimes we need to round a remainder up or down.

Example How many 3p sweets can you buy for 10p? 3 (with 1p left over)
How many four-seater tables are needed for 23 children? 6 tables (1 will have an empty space)

18 How many 12-packs of lollies are needed for 265 children?

19 How many 25p stamps can you buy for £2·70?

20 If 6 cakes fit in a box, how many boxes are needed for 50 cakes?

21 How many 52-seater coaches are needed for 250 passengers?

22 How many £2·35 burgers can you buy for £20·00?

23 How many 12-packs of pencils are needed to give 28 children two each?

24 A garage has 162 new tyres. How many cars can have 4 each?

Challenge

Make up some rounding up and rounding down division stories of your own.

Problems 6

1 Father Christmas wants to pack presents into boxes
so that they fit into his sleigh. He has to choose
just one size of box so that he can stack them up.
If he has 120 presents to pack, how many boxes of
each size would he fill completely?
   (a) Size A holds three toys.
   (b) Size B holds four toys.
   (c) Size C holds five toys.
   (d) Size D holds six toys.
   (e) Size E holds seven toys.
   (f) Size F holds eight toys.
   (g) Which box size would leave a toy left over?

2 A group of Manchester United fans have come to
Earth from a distant planet.
   They go in the club shop to buy souvenirs.
   (a) They have three identical feet each.
      How many football boots will 12 aliens need?
   (b) How many **pairs** of socks will six aliens need?
   (c) For dinner, nine aliens bought a box of 48 pies.
      How many of them would get an extra pie?
   (d) They each have three heads. They share out a
      box of 100 cheap woolly hats from the market.
      How many aliens can wear one on each of their
      three heads?
   (e) How many taxis will they need for 53 aliens to
      get to their spaceship if they can fit 6 in each taxi?

3 The five staff at *Cut Backs Hair Stylists* share the tips they get each day.
   If they have a remainder, they add it on to the next day's total.
   (a) How much did they take home each day?

Monday	£24·05
Tuesday	£47·32
Wednesday	£56·30
Thursday	£34·13
Friday	£78·39
Saturday	£124·51

   (b) Did they have a remainder left over at the end of the week?

Quick Multiplication

If you need to multiply a number by a multiple of 10, you can do it this way:

Example $7 \times 60 = (7 \times 6) \times 10 = 420$

1 $8 \times 40 =$

2 $4 \times 80 =$

3 $90 \times 2 =$

4 $7 \times 70 =$

5 $30 \times 6 =$

6 $60 \times 5 =$

If the larger number is even, you can halve it, multiply, then double the answer.

Example $8 \times 18 = (8 \times 9) \times 2 = 72 = 144$

Sometimes you can halve the larger number twice, then double the answer twice.

7 $8 \times 16 =$

8 $7 \times 32 =$

9 $4 \times 18 =$

10 $6 \times 14 =$

11 $36 \times 6 =$

12 $5 \times 26 =$

If the larger number is odd, subtract 1, halve, then add the smaller number.

Example 6×19 $6 \times 9 = 54$, double to 108, add the 6 = 114

13 $17 \times 6 =$

14 $9 \times 29 =$

15 $21 \times 7 =$

16 $5 \times 27 =$

17 $19 \times 4 =$

18 $8 \times 23 =$

With small numbers, halve one number and double the other before multiplying.

Example $18 \times 4 = 9 \times 8 = 72$

19 $4 \times 16 =$

20 $18 \times 3 =$

21 $14 \times 4 =$

Another way is to partition the larger number into tens and units, multiply by the tens, multiply by the units and add the answers together.

Example $63 \times 7 =$ $6 \times 7 = 42$, $42 \times 10 = 420$ $3 \times 7 = 21$ $420 + 21 = 441$

22 $6 \times 53 =$

23 $72 \times 8 =$

24 $34 \times 7 =$

Challenge

Make up ten equations, using one number less than 11 and the other between 10 and 100. Decide which method would be best, and try it out.

Swap your equations with a partner, and compare the methods you used.

Multiplying by 6, 7, 8 and 9

Complete the following.

1 $7 \times 7 =$

2 $7 \times 9 =$

3 $8 \times 8 =$

4 $8 \times 6 =$

5 $6 \times 6 =$

6 $9 \times 9 =$

7 $6 \times 7 =$

8 $8 \times 9 =$

9 $7 \times 8 =$

If you want to find 12, 14, 16, 18 or 20 times a number, you can multiply by 6, 7, 8, 9 or 10 and then double the answer, like in Unit 37.

Example 9×14 $9 \times 7 = 63$ and double to 126

Use this method to find these answers quickly.

10 $14 \times 6 =$

11 $8 \times 16 =$

12 $20 \times 9 =$

13 $7 \times 18 =$

14 $16 \times 7 =$

15 $6 \times 18 =$

To multiply by 11, 13, 15, 17 or 19, multiply by one less (10, 12, 14, 16 or 18), use the halving method, then add the smaller number, like in Unit 37.

Use this method to complete the following equations.

16 $7 \times 13 =$

17 $15 \times 8 =$

18 $7 \times 19 =$

19 $17 \times 9 =$

20 $8 \times 19 =$

21 $17 \times 7 =$

Now work out these equations, using one of the two halving methods.

22 $9 \times 14 =$

23 $21 \times 7 =$

24 $7 \times 12 =$

25 $8 \times 14 =$

26 $17 \times 6 =$

27 $19 \times 9 =$

28 $6 \times 20 =$

29 $17 \times 8 =$

30 $6 \times 21 =$

Challenge

Work out another easy way of multiplying by 11, 15 and 19.
Try it out. If it works, write down instructions and explain how it works to a partner.

Multiplication and Division 2

Dividing is the opposite operation of multiplying. If you know your multiplication facts, you also know your division facts.

Example $6 \times 7 = 42$, so $42 \div 6 = 7$ and $42 \div 7 = 6$

Write the multiplication facts that relate to these divisions.

1   $24 \div 6 =$

2   $90 \div 10 =$

3   $24 \div 4 =$

4   $16 \div 2 =$

5   $15 \div 3 =$

6   $63 \div 9 =$

7   $81 \div 9 =$

8   $36 \div 4 =$

9   $72 \div 9 =$

10   $49 \div 7 =$

11   $54 \div 6 =$

12   $24 \div 3 =$

13   $35 \div 5 =$

14   $48 \div 8 =$

15   $32 \div 8 =$

Complete these equations.

16   $18 \div = 3$

17   $ \div 6 = 2$

18   $40 \div = 10$

19   $ \div 6 = 6$

20   $72 \div = 9$

21   $ \div 6 = 3$

22   $56 \div = 8$

23   $ \div 5 = 4$

24   $28 \div = 7$

25   $ \div 5 = 9$

26   $36 \div = 4$

27   $ \div 3 = 8$

28   $42 \div = 6$

29   $ \div 3 = 7$

30   $25 \div = 5$

Challenge

With a partner, write down a list of incomplete division equations like the ones in questions 16 to 30. Make sure you both have a copy.
On the count of 1, 2, 3, race each other to see who completes them correctly first.
Try again with another set of equations, perhaps with a different partner.
See who is the fastest in your group.

finish

Doubles and Trebles

Double the following two-digit numbers.

Tip If there is a decimal point, you need to keep it in the same position.

1 39	5 9·5	9 0·27
2 0·58	6 26	10 0·61
3 17	7 74	11 99
4 7·2	8 47	12 3·6

Treble these numbers.

13 25	16 18	19 36
14 14	17 28	20 45
15 33	18 42	21 39

When you are doubling numbers that end with zero(s), it is easier if you remove the zero(s), do the doubling and then put the zero(s) back.

Example Double 350 Remove the zero, double 35 is 70, replace the zero = 700.
Double these numbers.

22 335	25 950	28 8650
23 50	26 750	29 1850
24 385	27 255	30 4450

Challenge

Choose a multiple of 5, double it and keep on doubling it until you reach over 10 000. How many doublings did it take?
Choose another multiple of 5 and predict how many doublings it will take to get to over 10 000.
Now test your prediction by doing it.
Try the same with a few more.
Predict and double with some multiples of 50.

Quick Halves

Halve these numbers.

If there is a decimal point, you need to keep it in the same position. If the number ends with an even digit followed by a zero (for example, 480, 3840), you can remove the zero, halve the remaining number and then put the zero back.

Example   Halve 3560
Remove the zero, half of 356 is 178, replace the zero = 1780.

1	180	11	1900	21	2200
2	1500	12	0·64	22	0·78
3	0·86	13	700	23	320
4	6·4	14	260	24	880
5	340	15	6800	25	480
6	8·2	16	1·48	26	6000
7	1200	17	1300	27	2·8
8	4·6	18	640	28	1400
9	110	19	5200	29	1·76
10	960	20	3·8	30	170

Challenge

Choose a large even number and keep on halving until you reach an odd number.
How many halvings did it take?
Try again, starting with a larger even number.
Can you choose a number that will give more halvings than a partner's number?

Problems 7

Priory School is ordering stock for next year.

1. How many individual items will they get if they buy:
   (a) 8 boxes of 1250 paper clips
   (b) 20 packs of 48 Maths exercise books
   (c) 15 packs of 25 English exercise books
   (d) 50 packs of 12 pencils
   (e) 24 packs of 18 handwriting pens
   (f) 12 packs of 6 pairs of scissors
   (g) 150 reams of A4 paper (a ream contains 500 sheets)
   (h) 8 boxes of 10 000 size 26 staples
   (i) 6 boxes of 5000 size 10 staples
   (j) 12 packs of 24 folders?

2. They expect each Year 5 child to use 3 English books and 4 Maths books in a year.
   (a) How many English books will a class of 12 boys and 17 girls need?
   (b) How many Maths books will the same Year 5 class need?
   (c) The other Year 5 class has 16 boys and 14 girls. How many Maths books do they need?
   (d) How many English books do they need?

3. Last year they ordered too many of some books, so they are halving this year's order.
   (a) Last year they bought 750 History books. How many will they buy this year?
   (b) Last year they bought 1140 Science books. How many will they buy this year?
   (c) Last year they bought 770 Geography books. How many will they buy this year?
   (d) Last year they bought 1350 work books. How many will they buy this year?

4. Last year they ran out of some things. How many will they buy if:
   (a) they triple last year's order for 36 packs of pencil crayons
   (b) they triple last year's order for 48 rolls of sticky tape
   (c) they triple last year's order for 38 sets of thin coloured felt pens
   (d) they triple last year's order for 17 sets of thick coloured felt pens?

Short-cuts (× and ÷) 1

Multiplication: if one number is a larger, even number, halve it and double the smaller number.

Example   5 × 18 → Double the 5 and halve the 18. 10 × 9 = 90

Work out the answers to all of these in your head.

1 7 × 18 =   **3** 3 × 18 =   **5** 6 × 20 =

2 4 × 14 =   **4** 9 × 16 =   **6** 12 × 9 =

Division: if both numbers are even, halve both and the answer stays the same.

Example   96 ÷ 8 = 12   Halve them both   48 ÷ 4 = 12

7 108 ÷ 18 =   **9** 162 ÷ 18 =   **11** 144 ÷ 16 =

8 132 ÷ 12 =   **10** 168 ÷ 14 =   **12** 126 ÷ 14 =

Both: you can halve one number then double the answer.

Example   24 × 7 = (12 × 7) × 2 = 168

13 160 ÷ 8 =   **16** 16 × 7 =   **19** 108 ÷ 6 =   **22** 54 ÷ 3 =

14 7 × 18 =   **17** 112 ÷ 7 =   **20** 18 × 9 =   **23** 64 ÷ 4 =

15 14 × 8 =   **18** 128 ÷ 8 =   **21** 5 × 14 =   **24** 22 × 7 =

Both: if one number is divisible by 4, halve it twice, then double the answer twice.

25 252 ÷ 7 =   **27** 192 ÷ 4 =   **29** 324 ÷ 9 =

26 32 × 6 =   **28** 36 × 5 =   **30** 24 × 8 =

Challenge

With a partner make up and agree five multiplications similar to these.
Agree on who uses which short-cut and have a race to see who gets the correct answers first.
Swap short-cuts and try again with five new multiplications.
Is one short-cut faster or is one partner faster?
Test a couple of division shortcuts the same way.

Multiplying Using Tens and Units

Here is a good easy way to multiply two-digit numbers in your head.

Example $26 \times 4 \rightarrow$ Partition the 26 into tens and units. 20 + 6
Now multiply 20 by 4 and 6 by 4 and add the two together.
$26 \times 4 = (20 \times 4) + (6 \times 4) = 80 + 24 = 104$

Use this method to work out these in your head.

1   $28 \times 5 =$

2   $32 \times 4 =$

3   $41 \times 2 =$

4   $56 \times 6 =$

5   $3 \times 36 =$

6   $53 \times 4 =$

7   $7 \times 64 =$

8   $82 \times 6 =$

9   $8 \times 58 =$

10   $75 \times 8 =$

11   $49 \times 7 =$

12   $64 \times 5 =$

13   $9 \times 44 =$

14   $9 \times 72 =$

15   $39 \times 8 =$

16   $7 \times 27 =$

17   $37 \times 4 =$

18   $6 \times 68 =$

19   $47 \times 4 =$

20   $6 \times 38 =$

21   $53 \times 3 =$

22   $46 \times 6 =$

23   $4 \times 42 =$

24   $73 \times 8 =$

25   $7 \times 39 =$

26   $48 \times 3 =$

27   $7 \times 34 =$

28   $61 \times 5 =$

29   $94 \times 6 =$

30   $97 \times 9 =$

Challenge

With one or two partners, choose four two-digit numbers and four numbers between 2 and 9.
Each of you should copy the numbers down in two columns.

Example   72   5
               45   2
               39   7
               19   4

In your head, multiply each two-digit number by each of the one-digit numbers.
On the count of 3 you all start, writing down only your answers.
When one of you finishes, the others must stop.
Check your answers together, working them out on paper or using a calculator.
The winner is the one with most correct answers.

Multiplying Using Factors

Here is another way to multiply two-digit numbers mentally. It does not work for 'prime numbers' (see Unit 10). Find a pair of factors of the two-digit number, multiply by the larger factor and then multiply the answer by the smaller factor.

Example $24 \times 9 \rightarrow$ Using 3 and 8 as factors, $8 \times 9 = 72, 72 \times 3 = 216$

Use this method to work out these in your head – sometimes there are more than one way.

1 $3 \times 36 =$

2 $24 \times 5 =$

3 $7 \times 25 =$

4 $9 \times 21 =$

5 $32 \times 3 =$

6 $5 \times 42 =$

7 $8 \times 36 =$

8 $18 \times 6 =$

9 $30 \times 6 =$

10 $18 \times 5 =$

11 $10 \times 60 =$

12 $16 \times 7 =$

13 $18 \times 9 =$

14 $2 \times 96 =$

15 $24 \times 8 =$

16 $4 \times 40 =$

17 $6 \times 22 =$

18 $28 \times 4 =$

19 $84 \times 2 =$

20 $8 \times 15 =$

21 $5 \times 33 =$

22 $56 \times 10 =$

23 $3 \times 27 =$

24 $45 \times 8 =$

25 $7 \times 48 =$

26 $42 \times 6 =$

27 $4 \times 36 =$

28 $9 \times 35 =$

29 $54 \times 4 =$

30 $27 \times 9 =$

Challenge

You need a partner to do this challenge.
Each of you should copy down these two columns of numbers:

39	6
53	4
84	9
91	8

One of you is going to use this 'factors' method of multiplying two-digit numbers in your head. The other is going to use the partitioning method (see Unit 44).
In your head, multiply each two-digit number by each of the one-digit numbers.
On the count of 3 you both start, writing down only your answers.
When one of you finishes, the others must stop.
Check your answers together, working them out on paper or using a calculator.
The winner is the one with more correct answers.

Multiples and Near Multiples of 10

Sometimes we need to multiply a number by a multiple of 10 (20, 30, 40, 50, 60, 70 and so on). The easy way is to split it up.

Example 8×30 $\quad$ 30 is 3×10, so: $3 \times 8 = 24$, $24 \times 10 = 240$
It also works the other way around.

If you are multiplying by 50, there is a quicker way. Because 50 is half of 100, simply multiply by 100, adding two zeros, then halve the answer.

Example 37×50 $\quad$ $37 \times 100 = 3700$, then halve the answer to 1850

Use these methods to work out the answers in your head.

1 $6 \times 40 =$
2 $8 \times 30 =$
3 $7 \times 70 =$
4 $90 \times 6 =$

5 $8 \times 20 =$
6 $8 \times 60 =$
7 $7 \times 50 =$
8 $5 \times 80 =$

9 $50 \times 5 =$
10 $30 \times 9 =$
11 $9 \times 40 =$
12 $40 \times 7 =$

13 $60 \times 6 =$
14 $70 \times 6 =$
15 $80 \times 8 =$

If you are multiplying by a number that is a 'near multiple' of 10 (nearly 20, 30, 40, 50 and so on), you can round it to the multiple and adjust the answer afterwards.

Example $19 \times 7 =$ $\quad$ Multiply 7 by 20 $\quad$ $7 \times 2 = 14$, $14 \times 10 = 140$
then adjust by subtracting one 7 $\quad$ $140 - 7 = 133$

$31 \times 8 =$ $\quad$ Multiply 8 by 30 $\quad$ $8 \times 3 = 24$, $24 \times 10 = 240$
then adjust by adding one 8 on $\quad$ $240 + 8 = 248$

Use this 'near multiple' method to work out these answers in your head.

16 $5 \times 41 =$
17 $3 \times 89 =$
18 $9 \times 61 =$
19 $6 \times 79 =$

20 $6 \times 71 =$
21 $6 \times 49 =$
22 $8 \times 69 =$
23 $7 \times 31 =$

24 $9 \times 19 =$
25 $7 \times 59 =$
26 $5 \times 81 =$
27 $6 \times 51 =$

28 $7 \times 29 =$
29 $8 \times 91 =$
30 $7 \times 39 =$

Challenge

Can you use this 'near multiple' method for numbers that are 2 more or 2 less than a multiple?
Give yourself a few equations like the examples below and see if you can work them out in your head.

$9 \times 32 =$ $\quad$ $8 \times 48 =$

Short-cuts (× and ÷) 2

To multiply a number:
- by 4 or 8, double the number twice or three times
- by 6, multiply by 3 and double the answer
- by 10, add a zero to push the digits one column to the left
- by 9, multiply by 10, adding a zero, then subtract 1 × the number
- by 11 or 12, multiply by 10, adding a zero, then add 1 or 2 × the number
- by 20, add a zero (as for 10 ×), then double the answer
- by 19 or 21, multiply by 20 (as above) and subtract or add 1 × the number
- by 100, add 2 zeros to push the digits two columns to the left
- by 50, add 2 zeros to push the digits two columns to the left, then halve the answer.

1   $25 \times 6 =$
2   $19 \times 7 =$
3   $12 \times 4 =$
4   $2 \times 36 =$
5   $24 \times 8 =$

6   $22 \times 6 =$
7   $8 \times 20 =$
8   $49 \times 11 =$
9   $21 \times 9 =$
10 $26 \times 5 =$

11 $4 \times 31 =$
12 $41 \times 4 =$
13 $46 \times 3 =$
14 $6 \times 19 =$
15 $33 \times 9 =$

16 $7 \times 21 =$
17 $4 \times 23 =$
18 $75 \times 8 =$

To divide a number:
- by 4 or 8, halve then halve again, or twice more
- by 6, divide by 3 then halve the answer; or halve and then divide the answer by 3
- by 9, divide by 3 then divide the answer by 3 again
- by 10, move the digits right one column – you may need a decimal point
- by 5, divide by 10 (as above), then double the answer
- by 100 move the digits right two columns – you may need a decimal point
- by 50, divide by 100 (as above), then double the answer.

19 $120 \div 4 =$
20 $750 \div 10 =$
21 $280 \div 4 =$
22 $1900 \div 50 =$

23 $180 \div 5 =$
24 $296 \div 8 =$
25 $215 \div 10 =$
26 $279 \div 9 =$

27 $1248 \div 100 =$
28 $168 \div 6 =$
29 $1650 \div 50 =$
30 $126 \div 6 =$

Challenge

Check a few of your multiplications by dividing the answer by one of the factors.
Check a few of your divisions by multiplying the answer.

Multiplying with Decimals

Use the short-cuts from Unit 47 to work out
these in your head. Take care with the decimals.

1 $13.5 \times 4 =$

2 $22 \times 9 =$

3 $26 \times 10 =$

4 $42.5 \times 20 =$

5 $2.2 \times 100 =$

6 $2.6 \times 6 =$

7 $6.25 \times 8 =$

8 $52 \times 4 =$

9 $2.1 \times 21 =$

10 $27 \times 5 =$

11 $6.2 \times 50 =$

12 $52 \times 9 =$

13 $5.3 \times 11 =$

14 $46 \times 19 =$

15 $3.2 \times 6 =$

16 $3.8 \times 6 =$

17 $24 \times 8 =$

18 $66 \times 20 =$

19 $225 \times 21 =$

20 $7.5 \times 100 =$

21 $25.3 \times 4 =$

22 $19.5 \times 9 =$

23 $24.4 \times 10 =$

24 $32.7 \times 50 =$

25 $26.5 \times 19 =$

26 $26.2 \times 5 =$

27 $125 \times 11 =$

28 $49 \times 6 =$

29 $12.4 \times 8 =$

30 $57 \times 5 =$

Challenge

Choose a starting number less than 10 that has a decimal in it (for example, 7·4).
Multiply it in your head by a number less than 6.
Does the answer have a decimal in it? If it has, multiply it by another number.
Keep on multiplying the answer until you don't have a decimal in the answer.
Use the same starting number and try again, beginning by multiplying by a
different number.
Are some numbers better for getting rid of the decimal part than others?

Problems 8

Derek the odd-job man can only do things by halves.

1 He was asked to trim a hedge that had grown
to 3·84 metres high.
  (a) He trimmed off half its height.
    How tall was it now?
  (b) The customer asked him to do it another
    four times. Each time Derek trimmed off
    half of its height. How tall was it when he
    had finished?

2 Derek planted 24 tulip bulbs, but the customer wanted more.
  (a) He fetched half as many again and added them to the
    others that he had planted. How many were planted so far?
  (b) The customer still wasn't happy, so Derek fetched more –
    half of the total already planted. How many had he planted now?
  (c) Derek had one last go at making the customer happy.
    He fetched more bulbs – the same number as half the total
    already planted. What is the total number of bulbs planted?
  (d) Why couldn't Derek plant half the amount again?

3 **(a)** On Monday Derek worked for eight hours at £6 per hour. How much did
    he earn?
  (b) On Tuesday the customer wasn't happy and halved Derek's hourly rate of
    pay. How much did he earn in eight hours on Tuesday?
  (c) Wednesday was no better – the
    customer halved his rate of pay
    again. How much did he earn in
    eight hours on Wednesday?
  (d) On Thursday, Derek's pay
    was cut in half again. How
    much did he earn for eight
    hours' work on Thursday?
  (e) On Friday Derek quit his job,
    after he received another
    halving of his pay. How
    much did he earn in 8 hours
    on Friday?

Multiplying on Paper

When we multiply tens and units by units,
we usually set it out like this: multiply the units,
then multiply the tens. Add on the 2 tens
from below the line. Write the 4 tens in the answer line
and exchange 10 tens to below the line in the hundreds column.

```
  4 5 3 7
×       4
─────────
      4 8
    1 2
```

Now multiply the hundreds and add on the 1 hundred from
below the line. Write the 1 hundred in the answer
line and exchange the 20 hundreds to the thousands column.

Finally, multiply the thousands and add on the 2 hundreds
from below the line.

```
  4 5 3 7
×       4
─────────
1 8 1 4 8
  2 1 2
```

Use this method to work these out.

1. 353 × 4
6. 863 × 5
11. 6241 × 3
16. 3453 × 6
21. 1740 × 4
26. 3053 × 6

2. 2648 × 3
7. 3462 × 4
12. 1364 × 4
17. 4386 × 5
22. 1759 × 6
27. 4536 × 5

3. 743 × 5
8. 734 × 3
13. 2551 × 6
18. 5132 × 3
23. 4852 × 3
28. 5309 × 3

4. 5361 × 6
9. 2745 × 6
14. 3214 × 8
19. 3768 × 5
24. 3895 × 2
29. 3738 × 5

5. 6438 × 6
10. 945 × 8
15. 2494 × 5
20. 4634 × 8
25. 3401 × 8
30. 4764 × 8

Challenge

Choose a two-digit number and multiply it by a one-digit number.
Now multiply the answer by the one-digit number.
Keep on multiplying the answer by the one-digit number until you get to over 1000.
How many multiplyings did it take?
Try again with two new starting numbers – will it take the same number of goes?

50

Multiplying a Decimal on Paper

When we multiply using decimal numbers, we can use the same method as for whole numbers. The only difference is that we have to put in a decimal point to separate the whole numbers from the decimals. To multiply with decimals set it out like this. Put the decimal point in the answer line before you start. Make sure that it is beneath the decimal point in the number you are multiplying, and between the units and the $\frac{1}{10}$ column.

$$
\begin{array}{r}
\text{H T U} \quad \frac{1}{10} \; \frac{1}{100} \\
2\;4\;\cdot\;2\;\;5 \\
\times \qquad 7\;\cdot \\
\hline
\cdot \qquad 5 \\
\hline
{}_{3}
\end{array}
$$

Use the method shown in Unit 50. Make sure you put the first answer numerals (for 7×0.05) in the $\frac{1}{100}$ column, then exchange in the usual way.

Use this method to work these out.

1	6·32 × 2	**6**	24·47 × 3	**11**	39·60 × 9	**16**	73·84 × 7	**21**	258·25 × 7
2	8·24 × 5	**7**	35·35 × 9	**12**	57·65 × 2	**17**	99·99 × 5	**22**	325·55 × 4
3	10·75 × 3	**8**	37·42 × 6	**13**	84·23 × 5	**18**	58·08 × 9	**23**	206·45 × 8
4	18·51 × 7	**9**	29·66 × 8	**14**	52·95 × 4	**19**	152·95 × 4	**24**	259·86 × 6
5	14·85 × 4	**10**	20·78 × 2	**15**	68·74 × 8	**20**	162·45 × 3	**25**	167·02 × 9

Challenge

Go back to these multiplications and make estimates of what the answer should be.

Example 39·60 × 9 Round up to 40 × 10. The answer should be just under 400. It can be useful to make estimates like this **before** you work out the answer.

Long Multiplication

We can multiply by numbers with two digits or more using **long multiplication**. Set it out like this example, with two blank lines beneath the numbers and another line beneath those for totalling up the final answer.

```
    H T U
    2 5 8
×     3 4
  7 7 4 0
  1 0 3 2
  8 7 7 2
```

First multiply by the tens. You do this by putting a zero in the units column to push the numerals to the left, then carry on as you did in Unit 50. There is no space to write down any exchanging, so you have to use your memory! Now beneath it, multiply by the units. Finally, add the total of the two answers. You can use the space below the bottom line to exchange when you add up.

Use this method to work out these.

1	46 × 23	**6**	67 × 45	**11**	68 × 85	**16**	154 × 48	**21**	325 × 53
2	38 × 29	**7**	72 × 52	**12**	76 × 64	**17**	174 × 36	**22**	386 × 57
3	67 × 34	**8**	78 × 48	**13**	78 × 59	**18**	248 × 28	**23**	416 × 68
4	53 × 41	**9**	97 × 38	**14**	95 × 93	**19**	267 × 38	**24**	637 × 72
5	86 × 37	**10**	89 × 43	**15**	87 × 86	**20**	209 × 49	**25**	754 × 65

Challenge

Use rounding up and down and make estimates of what some of your answers **could** be.

Example   89 × 43   Round up to 90 × 40 = 360 and add a zero.
The answer should be near to 3600.
It is useful to make estimates like this **before** you work out the answer.

Dividing on Paper

When we divide, we work from the largest column (on the left) to the smallest.

Example   First divide the 3 hundreds.

$$3 \overline{) 3\ 9\ 6}$$ with quotient 1

Next divide the 9 tens.

$$3 \overline{) 3\ 9\ 6}$$ with quotient $1\ 3$

Finally divide the 6 units.

$$3 \overline{) 3\ 9\ 6}$$ with quotient $1\ 3\ 2$

Try these.

1	$3 \overline{) 6\ 0\ 9}$
2	$4 \overline{) 8\ 8\ 8\ 0}$
3	$6 \overline{) 6\ 6\ 0\ 6}$
4	$2 \overline{) 6\ 2\ 8\ 4}$
5	$5 \overline{) 5\ 0\ 5\ 5}$
6	$3 \overline{) 6\ 9\ 3\ 6}$

If you get a remainder, 'carry it on' to the next column. $3 \overline{) 5\ ^2 4\ 6}$ with quotient $1\ 8\ 2$

If the number is too small to divide into, carry it all to the next column. $4 \overline{) 2\ ^2 4\ 8}$ with quotient $0\ 6\ 2$

7	$2 \overline{) 4\ 7\ 6}$	11	$8 \overline{) 6\ 6\ 4}$	15	$6 \overline{) 3\ 4\ 4\ 4}$	19	$5 \overline{) 9\ 3\ 7\ 0}$	23	$4 \overline{) 9\ 9\ 7\ 2}$	27	$4 \overline{) 8\ 7\ 3\ 2}$
8	$6 \overline{) 3\ 8\ 4}$	12	$4 \overline{) 9\ 7\ 6}$	16	$2 \overline{) 6\ 1\ 3\ 8}$	20	$8 \overline{) 5\ 2\ 2\ 4}$	24	$2 \overline{) 7\ 9\ 1\ 6}$	28	$8 \overline{) 7\ 7\ 7\ 6}$
9	$5 \overline{) 7\ 3\ 5}$	13	$7 \overline{) 4\ 5\ 5}$	17	$5 \overline{) 7\ 6\ 1\ 5}$	21	$9 \overline{) 9\ 9\ 5\ 4}$	25	$3 \overline{) 8\ 5\ 8\ 6}$	29	$6 \overline{) 9\ 1\ 0\ 8}$
10	$3 \overline{) 2\ 9\ 7}$	14	$9 \overline{) 8\ 6\ 4}$	18	$7 \overline{) 1\ 1\ 4\ 8}$	22	$3 \overline{) 8\ 8\ 0\ 8}$	26	$7 \overline{) 8\ 3\ 0\ 2}$	30	$9 \overline{) 8\ 1\ 6\ 3}$

Challenge

Choose two rows of divisions and check your answers by multiplying your answer by the number you divided by.
If you've got it right (and your multiplying is correct), you should end up with the number you divided.

Dividing Decimals

In Unit 53 you were dividing three- and four-digit numbers.
We use the same method to divide numbers with decimals.
Before you start to divide, make sure that you put the
decimal point in the answer space, above the decimal point
in the number you are dividing.

Try these.

$4\overline{)7\cdot44}$

1 $3\overline{)6\cdot96}$ **2** $4\overline{)80\cdot96}$ **3** $6\overline{)6\cdot06}$ **4** $2\overline{)26\cdot46}$ **5** $5\overline{)55\cdot50}$ **6** $3\overline{)36\cdot99}$

If you get a remainder, 'carry it on' to the next column. $6\overline{)8\cdot^{2}4\,6}^{\,1\cdot81}$

If the number is too small to divide into, carry it all to the next column. $4\overline{)2\cdot^{2}4\,8}^{\,0\cdot62}$

Try these. You will need to 'carry' some remainders on to the next column.

7 $3\overline{)21\cdot6}$ **11** $4\overline{)7\cdot52}$ **15** $3\overline{)73\cdot47}$ **19** $9\overline{)29\cdot61}$ **23** $7\overline{)94\cdot64}$ **27** $9\overline{)70\cdot47}$

8 $5\overline{)5\cdot45}$ **12** $9\overline{)4\cdot86}$ **16** $7\overline{)54\cdot04}$ **20** $2\overline{)135\cdot08}$ **24** $6\overline{)85\cdot68}$ **28** $4\overline{)94\cdot32}$

9 $2\overline{)23\cdot28}$ **13** $4\overline{)39\cdot16}$ **17** $6\overline{)38\cdot58}$ **21** $8\overline{)79\cdot28}$ **25** $7\overline{)60\cdot27}$ **29** $3\overline{)88\cdot89}$

10 $8\overline{)3\cdot52}$ **14** $8\overline{)91\cdot84}$ **18** $2\overline{)77\cdot56}$ **22** $5\overline{)49\cdot90}$ **26** $6\overline{)74\cdot34}$ **30** $5\overline{)92\cdot05}$

Challenge

Choose a row of divisions from this unit and check them by multiplying the
answer by the number you divided by. (Look back at Unit 51 to see how to
multiply with decimals.)

If you've got it right (and your multiplying is correct), you should end up with the
number you divided.

Problems 9

The end-of-year school disco was organised by Class 6. They decided not to let the teachers interfere with the plans. They went to the warehouse and to save time they split up into groups and met up at the check-out.
Here is what each group had:

Jill's group
12 packs of 24 cans of pop
6 boxes of 48 packs of crisps
38 packs of 12 choc ices
27 packs of 32 plain biscuits

Darren's group
100 packs of 12 choc ices
80 boxes of 36 packs of chewing gum

Kerry's group
64 packets of 18 custard cream biscuits
16 packs of 18 cartons of fruit juice
30 packs of 12 choc ices
24 packets of 24 chocolate biscuits
2 boxes of 72 cheese straws

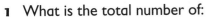

1   What is the total number of:
   (a) choc ices
   (b) plain biscuits
   (c) chocolate biscuits
   (d) packets of crisps
   (e) packs of chewing gum
   (f) custard cream biscuits
   (g) cartons of fruit juice
   (h) cans of pop
   (i) cheese straws?

2   There were 288 children at the party. Share out everything equally.
   What will each child get?

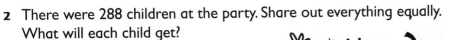

What's the Chance?

If we toss a coin up into the air:
- there is an **even chance** it will be 'heads'
- it is **unlikely** that it will land on its edge
- it is **certain** that it will fall
- it is **impossible** that it will float

We use words and phrases like those in the cloud to make predictions about how events may turn out.

> impossible, no chance
> even chance
> certain
>
> possible
> likely, good chance, probable

Choose words from the cloud to say what these chances are.

1. Throwing **(a)** an odd number, **(b)** a 6, **(c)** an 8 on one die?
2. Throwing a total score of **(a)** 2, **(b)** 4, **(c)** 7, **(d)** 10, **(e)** 14 on two dice?

The hardest predictions to make are those that are so **unlikely** that we think they are impossible, and those that are so **likely** that we think they are certain. Choose words from the cloud to describe these chances. Some answers will depend upon you, the weather, what day it is and other things that change.

3. you will go home today
4. you will stop in school all night
5. your teacher will bring you all a cake
6. you will see aliens on your way home
7. it will be a wet playtime
8. a boy will be first in line for dinner
9. someone will fall over at playtime
10. your teachers will win the lottery and retire
11. you will ask for extra homework
12. you will watch television tonight
13. your home will be struck by lightning
14. you will walk to school tomorrow
15. you will eat bread today
16. you will eat fish today
17. you will have a drink today
18. you will eat Christmas cake today
19. you will become prime minister today
20. you will become prime minister one day

Copy this scale line in your book, and use arrows to point to where the events in questions 3 to 20 would come.

←——— *less likely*   *more likely* ———→

| no chance | even | chance | certain |

Challenge

Make up some events of your own and use words and a scale line to predict the chances.

Bar Charts

Greg and Rachel have thrown two dice 100 times and have counted the frequency of each number thrown. The results are shown in the frequency chart.

total	frequency
1	0
2	1
3	3
4	4
5	6
6	15
7	42
8	11
9	10
10	5
11	2
12	1

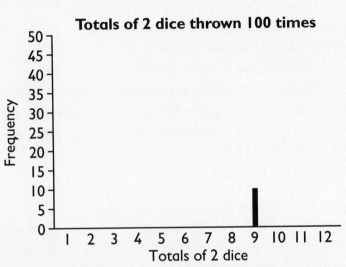

Totals of 2 dice thrown 100 times

1 Copy and complete the bar chart.

2 Which score is most frequent?

3 Explain why there is no score of 1.

4 List the scores in **descending** order of frequency (starting with the highest).

5 Explain **why** the most frequent score is the most frequent.

6 If you rolled a single die 60 times, what frequency would you expect for each score?

7 If you rolled it 120 times, what frequency would you expect for each score?

8 With a partner, roll a die 60 times and record your results on a bar chart.

9 How do the results compare with your prediction?

10 Roll the die another 60 times and again draw a bar chart of the results.

11 Compare the 2 charts. Are the results similar?

12 Put both sets of results together on to one chart (the results of all 120 throws). How do the results compare with your prediction?

Challenge

Roll two dice 72 times and make a frequency chart of the totals (like Greg and Rachel's).
Draw a bar chart of your results.
How do your results compare with what you might expect?

Venn and Carroll Diagrams

Here is a **Venn diagram**, which shows children who have hobbies. Each ring is labelled to tell us about the people inside it. People can be inside more than one ring, or, like Patrick, may not be in any. The names appear in eight groups.

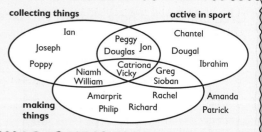

1 Write a short description for each of the eight groups of children to say what they do and don't do.

2 What doesn't Greg do?

3 What doesn't Chantel do?

4 What doesn't Richard do?

Here is a **Carroll diagram**, named after Lewis Carroll, writer of the famous 'Alice' books. It shows 25 children, grouped in columns according to their year group, and in rows according to what they do at dinnertime. Use the Carroll diagram to find the answers to these questions.

	Year 4	Year 5	Year 6
has school dinners	Amarprit Rachel Douglas Sioban	Philip Richard Lesley	Christopher Patrick Joseph Vicky
brings packed lunch	Chantel Greg	Dougal Ibrahim Hayley Luke	Niamh Poppy Peggy
goes home for dinner	Catriona Ian	Amanda	Jon William

5 How many children go home for dinner?

6 How many children stay in school for dinner?

7 How many children have a school dinner?

8 How many children bring a packed lunch?

9 Which Year 4 children have school dinners?

10 Who goes home for dinner from Year 5?

11 Make a Carroll diagram of your own using the children in your class. Sort them into columns for **boy** or **girl**, and into rows for **dark hair** or **light hair**.

Challenge

Make up another Carroll diagram, choosing how you sort the information for the columns and rows.

Mode, Median and Mean

The Year 6 children have just spent a week doing SATs practice tests. Here are their scores.

	English			Maths test 'A'	Maths test 'B'	Mental Maths	Science test 'A'	Science test 'B'
	Reading	Writing	Spelling					
Chris	15	28	17	38	32	12	29	28
Drew	35	36	19	33	33	13	29	30
Jon	8	14	7	15	12	5	20	18
Joseph	33	35	20	28	30	15	41	42
Niamh	29	32	20	36	37	12	31	28
Patrick	24	21	18	19	18	7	22	22
Peggy	26	28	15	33	31	14	29	25
Poppy	24	25	18	25	25	12	40	37
Vicky	24	23	16	31	35	18	43	39
William	32	28	20	22	27	12	36	31

For each test we could compare each child's score with:

- the mean. To find the mean, add up all the scores and divide by the number of scores. The Reading test score total is 250 and there are ten children's scores, so the mean is $250 \div 10 = 25$.
- the mode. This is simply the most common score in a category.
- the median. This is the middle score when the scores are written in order. If there are two middle scores, the median is the number exactly between them. For the Reading test there are 2 middle scores, 26 and 29, so the median has to be exactly half way between them, $27\frac{1}{2}$.

1 Find the mean, mode and median for each test.

2 (a) Who scored better than the mean in the Writing test? Who scored better than the mode? Who scored better than the median?

 (b) Who scored better than the mean in the Mental Maths test? Who scored better than the mode? Who scored better than the median?

3 Which method of comparing do you think works best for these data: the mean, mode or median?

Challenge

Add together each child's scores for the two Science tests.
Work out the mean, median and mode for the totalled scores.
Compare the children with the mean, mode and median. Which children do better?
Is it the same children who score better than each measurment?

Problems 10

Here are the results of a survey of which takeaway food the children like.

	Takeaway food we like to eat			
	curry	burgers	pizza	chips
Amanda	☺	☺		
Amarprit		☺		☺
Catriona		☺		☺
Chantel			☺	
Dougal	☺	☺	☺	☺
Douglas	☺		☺	
Greg	☺			☺
Hayley		☺		☺
Ian	☺	☺		☺
Ibrahim	☺		☺	☺
Lesley			☺	☺
Luke		☺		☺
Philip	☺	☺		
Rachel	☺			☺
Richard	☺		☺	☺
Sioban		☺		☺

1. Look back at the Venn and Carroll diagrams used in Unit 58. Which sort do you think would be better to show the takeaway food data?

2. Use the diagram of your choice to show these data.

3. Does it work? If it doesn't, try the other sort of diagram.

4. Make up five questions to go with your successful diagram, and include what the correct answers should be.

5. Total up how many children like each type of takeaway.

6. Add up the totals and find the mean, mode and median of the four totals. (You might need to look at Unit 59 to remind yourself of how to do this.)

Length, Mass and Capacity

We can measure length in kilometres (km), metres (m), centimetres (cm) and millimetres (ml).

We can measure mass (weight) in kilograms (kg) and grams (g).

We can measure volume and capacity in litres (l) and millilitres (ml).

Reminders   I kilogram = 1000 grams   I litre = 1000 millilitres

I kilometre = 1000 metres   I metre = 1000 millimetres

I metre = 100 centimetres

Complete these conversions.

1   $\frac{3}{10}$ kg = ⬭ g

2   $\frac{1}{5}$ l = ⬭ ml

3   $\frac{6}{10}$ m = ⬭ mm

4   2650 ml = ⬭ l

5   $\frac{1}{4}$ m = ⬭ mm

6   1200 g = ⬭ kg

7   $\frac{1}{2}$ m = ⬭ cm

8   $4\frac{1}{4}$ kg = ⬭ g

9   $\frac{3}{4}$ l = ⬭ ml

Many older people prefer to use the old **imperial** units of measurement. Here are some **approximate** conversions that can be used without a calculator.

Length   I inch is about $2\frac{1}{2}$ cm.   I foot (12 inches) is about 30 cm.

I yard (3 feet) is about I m and 9 cm.

Weight   I pound (symbol **lb**) is about 450g. I ounce is about 28 g.

Volume   I gallon (8 pints) is about $4\frac{1}{2}$ litres. I pint is just over $\frac{1}{2}$ of a litre.

Use these approximate conversions to change the following into metric units.

10 8 inches	16 10 yards	22 3 pints	28 4 ounces
11 5 inches	17 12 yards	23 6 pints	29 10 ounces
12 2 feet	18 $3\frac{1}{2}$ feet	24 10 pints	30 8 ounces
13 5 feet	19 2 gallons	25 2 lb	
14 I foot, 4 inches	20 10 gallons	26 $3\frac{1}{2}$ lb	
15 2 yards	21 44 gallons	27 8 lb	

Challenge

Use a calculator and these figures to make more accurate conversions.

Length   I inch = 2·54 cm   I foot = 0·3048 m   I yard = 0·9144 m

Weight   I ounce = 28·35 g   I lb = 0·4536 kg

Volume   I pint = 0·568 litres   I gallon = 4·546 litres

Now you know why the less accurate conversions are easier!

How Accurate?

When we measure, we don't always need to be exact. For example, distances marked on road signs are not accurate to the nearest metre. But some measurements need to be very accurate – to the nearest millimetre or even closer. Below are some things to be measured. Choose from the chart the units you would use to measure, and say how accurate you would wish to be.

length	weight	volume	time
kilometres (km) metres (m) centimetres (cm) millimetres (ml)	tonnes kilograms, kilos (kg) grams (g)	litres (l) millilitres (ml)	centuries, years months, weeks, days, hours, minutes (') seconds (")

Example '**I would measure a replacement window in millimetres to the nearest mm.**'

1 the distance between two goal posts
2 the distance between two towns
3 the length of pin
4 the thickness of a pencil lead
5 the length of a pencil
6 the weight of a packet of crisps
7 the weight of a dog
8 the weight of an elephant
9 the weight of a hamster
10 the water to fill a bath

11 the pop inside a glass
12 the medicine in a spoonful
13 the age of house
14 the age of a dinosaur skeleton
15 the age of your teacher (careful...!)
16 the age of a baby
17 the duration of playtime
18 the length of the school summer holiday
19 the duration of an English lesson
20 the time to run 100 metres

Check the markings on your ruler. Make sure that you have 10 mm marked between each cm.
Measure the following in mm to the nearest whole millimetre.

21 the length of a piece of A4 paper
22 the width of a piece of A4 paper
23 the length of this Ginn maths book
24 the width of this Ginn maths book
25 the thickness of this Ginn maths book

26 the length of your maths exercise book
27 the width of your maths exercise book
28 the width of your ruler
29 the length of your pencil
30 the width of your pencil

Challenge

Find a way of measuring the thickness of a piece of paper.

Area

Area is the amount of flat (two-dimensional) space that something occupies. We use 'square' units to measure area, such as square metres (m²), square centimetres (cm²) or even square millimetres (mm²). We use the little ² to mean 'square' because a square has two dimensions: length and width. The rectangle on the right is drawn with cm² marked on it. To find its area you could simply count the squares, but it is quicker to do it by multiplying.

length 6 cm

width 4 cm

We know that **area = length × breadth**, so we multiply like this:

6 cm × 4 cm = 24 cm²

When we give the measurements of a rectangle, we say '6 cm by 4 cm' and write **6 cm × 4 cm**.

Find the area of these rectangles. Take care with the units of measure – they are not all in cm.

1 a rectangle 6 cm wide and 8 cm long
2 a flowerbed 8 m long and 2 m wide
3 a sheet of card 30 cm long and 20 cm wide
4 an envelope 16 cm × 10 cm
5 a lawn 15 m × 8 m
6 an 8 cm square
7 a car park 50 m × 30 m

8 a playground 40 m long and 10 m wide
9 an envelope 24 cm × 16 cm
10 a table top 100 cm long and 60 cm wide
11 an atlas 45 cm × 30 cm
12 a notepad 14 cm × 9 cm
13 a postage stamp 22 mm × 19 mm
14 the top of a cube, 10 mm square

If you cut a rectangle in half diagonally, you will get two right-angled triangles. We can use this to find the area of right-angled triangles. We use the sides that form the right angle of a right-angled triangle, multiply them together and divide by 2: **(side 1 × side 2) ÷ 2. Don't use the longest side.**

Example   (5 cm × 4 cm) ÷ 2 = 20 cm² ÷ 2 = 10 cm²
Copy these triangles and find their areas.

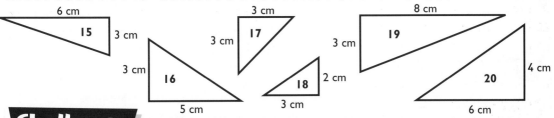

Challenge

Draw some more triangles and calculate their areas.

Perimeter

The **perimeter** of a shape is the distance all around its edge. With rectangles and triangles, the simplest way to find the perimeter is to add up the lengths of the sides.

Perimeter of triangle = side 1 + side 2 + side 3

Perimeter of rectangle = side1 + side 2 + side 3 + side 4

With rectangles, you can also use these two methods:

Perimeter of rectangle = (2 × length of rectangle) + (2 × width of rectangle)

Perimeter of rectangle = (length of rectangle + width of rectangle) × 2

With square rectangles, there is an even quicker way because all four sides are the same length.

Perimeter of square = length of 1 side × 4

Find the perimeters of these triangles.

	side 1	side 2	side 3		side 1	side 2	side 3		side 1	side 2	side 3
1	6 cm	5 cm	7 cm	6	9 cm	8 cm	7 cm	11	9 cm	4 cm	6 cm
2	10 cm	8 cm	6 cm	7	4 cm	8 cm	4 cm	12	3 cm	4 cm	11 cm
3	7 cm	14 cm	16 cm	8	5 cm	8 cm	4 cm	13	12 cm	10 cm	$8\frac{1}{2}$ cm
4	3 cm	7 cm	5 cm	9	5 cm	10 cm	13 cm	14	4 cm	$3\frac{1}{4}$ cm	$4\frac{1}{2}$ cm
5	6 cm	6 cm	8 cm	10	7 cm	4 cm	5 cm	15	$4\frac{3}{4}$ cm	$8\frac{1}{4}$ cm	$3\frac{1}{2}$ cm

Find the perimeters of these rectangles.

16 8 cm × 5 cm

17 9 m × 9 m

18 12 cm × 5 cm

19 20 m × 4 m

20 7 cm × 3 cm

21 12 m × 18 m

22 8 cm × 8 cm

23 25 m × 10 m

24 100 mm × 120 mm

25 120 mm × 120 mm

26 30 cm × 8 cm

27 $5\frac{1}{2}$ cm × 8 cm

28 $12\frac{1}{2}$ cm × $12\frac{1}{2}$ cm

29 $8\frac{1}{4}$ cm × $3\frac{3}{4}$ cm

30 $10\frac{1}{2}$ m × 15 m

Challenge

Find an easy way of working out the perimeters of these regular shapes:

a hexagon with sides 6 cm long

an octagon with sides 5 cm long

a heptagon with sides 4 cm long

a pentagon with sides 8 cm long

a decagon with sides 4 cm long.

1 The children in the nursery are wandering off across the field instead of staying close to the building. The headteacher has decided to fence off a rectangular area around the door of the nursery. She has 96 m of wire mesh.

(a) Draw four different ways she could make the rectangular pen with a perimeter of 96 m.

(b) Work out the area of each possible pen.

(c) What size of pen would have the smallest area (using whole metres)?

(d) What size of pen would have the largest area?

(e) What is the difference in area between the largest and the smallest?

2 The headteacher decided to have another area covered with rubber safety matting. She measured 30 m × 20 m, but on the telephone ordered 30 feet by 20 feet by mistake.

(a) Work out the area of matting she wanted in m².

(b) How many square feet of matting did she actually order?

(c) Convert the imperial sizes she gave on the telephone to exact metric measurements (see Unit 61 if you are not sure how to do this with a calculator).

(d) Use the conversions to work out how many m² of matting she ordered.

(e) Find the difference between the area of matting she meant to order and the area she actually ordered.

(f) Did she order too much or too little?

3 The school needed to order new carpet for some of the classrooms. The teachers banned the head from doing the measuring this time – the children did it instead. Work out the area of carpet needed, then add up the total area.

	Length of room	Width of room
Nursery	25 m	12 m
Reception	20 m	8 m
Class 1	16 m	10 m
Class 2	15 m	10 m
Class 3	18 m	10 m

Time and Timetables

When we write down or say the time, we use many ways. If it is exactly on the hour, we say **o'clock** (short for 'of the clock'). Sometimes we choose to record what **part of an hour** it is since the last hour or before the next. Or we might say **how many minutes** it is since the last hour or before the next.

We could say or record this clock's time as **quarter to 8, 15 minutes to 8, or 7:45.** This is a **12-hour** clock. When we reach an hour after the middle of the day, we have to start counting again at 1. The clock face doesn't say if it is before 12 noon (**a.m.**) or after 12 noon (**p.m.**). To say which we mean, we add on a.m. or p.m.

An easier, neater way to record the time is the **24-hour clock**. We carry on counting the hours so that 1 p.m. becomes 13:00, 2 p.m. becomes 14:00 and so on. To keep it simple, we just write down the hour and the minutes past the hour in two digits with a colon in between: **07:45**.

If the time is p.m. in the 12-hour clock, we add 12 to the hours.

Change these times to 24-hour clock times.

Example   quarter past 7 p.m. = 19:15

1 9 o'clock a.m.	**6** quarter to 8 p.m.	**11** 20 to 5 a.m.	**16** 1 minute to midnight
2 7:15 p.m.	**7** 12 noon	**12** 25 past 6 p.m.	**17** 1 minute past midnight
3 half past 3 p.m.	**8** 10:30 a.m.	**13** 10 to 7 a.m.	**18** quarter to 1 a.m.
4 quarter past 7 a.m.	**9** 9:30 a.m.	**14** 10 past 7 a.m.	**19** $\frac{1}{4}$ past 1 p.m.
5 20 past 5 p.m.	**10** 5 to 11 p.m.	**15** 9:45 p.m.	**20** 1 minute past 8 p.m.

Here is part of a train timetable, written in the 24-hour clock. Convert the times into 12-hour clock times.

depart	09:35	11:05	13:45	15:20	18:55
arrive	10:53	12:23	15:03	16:38	20:15

Challenge

Think about the times of the day that are important to you (when you get up, eat, do things, etc.).

Write down these events and times using both 12- and 24-hour clocks.

Time Intervals

The simplest way of calculating an interval of
time is to **count on**, using 24-hour clock times.

Example   09:35 to 12:20
09:35 + **25** minutes = 10:00
10:00 + **2** hours = 12:00
12:00 + **20** minutes = 12:20
2 hours + 25 minutes + 20 minutes = **2 hours, 45 minutes.**
Use this way to work out these time intervals.

1 09:30 to 10:15	**6** 10:45 to 16:35	**11** 09:50 to 22:10
2 10:30 to 11:30	**7** 19:20 to 21:25	**12** 07:15 to 23:05
3 07:10 to 11:25	**8** 20:15 to 23:05	**13** 08:23 to 10:42
4 11:20 to 15:30	**9** 18:40 to 22:20	**14** 11:47 to 13:38
5 09:40 to 18:15	**10** 17:05 to 17:55	**15** 15:17 to 20:39

Here is a different way of working out time intervals. Subtract the earlier time
from the later time like this. If the minutes in the later time are less than the
earlier time, you need to exchange one hour for 60 minutes.

Example 10:50 to 15:20	hours	minutes
Exchange one hour.	14	+60
Subtract the 50 from the 60 = 10	1̶5̶	20
Add on to the 20 = 30 minutes	−10	50
Subtract the hours.	4	**30**

Use this subtraction method to work out these time intervals.

16 06:20 to 10:30	**21** 09:45 to 12:35	**26** 08:42 to 14:43
17 08:15 to 11:55	**22** 17:25 to 20:10	**27** 09:13 to 21:05
18 09:15 to 13:45	**23** 21:15 to 22:00	**28** 08:29 to 10:56
19 12:40 to 14:30	**24** 15:27 to 18:52	**29** 11:47 to 13:38
20 06:30 to 08:15	**25** 16:05 to 22:38	**30** 06:56 to 23:50

Challenge

How could you alter this subtraction method to find intervals of time that go into
the next day: for example, 22:30 on Monday to 03:40 on Tuesday?
Try it out.
Now use the 'counting on' method to check if your way works.
Explain your method to a friend and write out instructions on how to do it.

Problems 12

1 This is how Mika the cat spent part of a day:
07:30 he came in after a night outside in the rain
07:30 till 07:35 he was drying himself off by lying on
Alison's new quilt cover
07:35 till 08:10 he was meowing and looking
for someone to feed him
08:10 till 08:13 he spent eating
08:14 till 11:50 he was sleeping on top
of the ironing
11:51 till 12:07 he asked to be fed again
12:08 till 12:10 he was eating
12:11 till 17:30 he was outside
'hunting'
17:31 till 19:40 he was asleep on
the central
heating boiler
19:41 till 20:10 he asked for more food
20:11 till 20:13 he was eating

Work out how long Mika spent:
   (a) hunting
   (b) sleeping
   (c) asking for food
   (d) eating
   (e) lying on a bed.

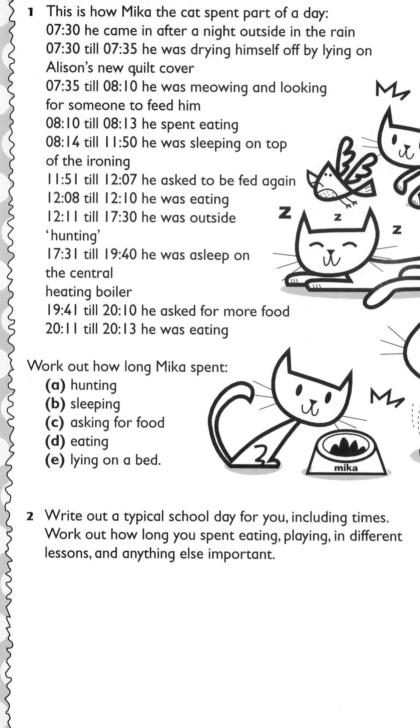

2 Write out a typical school day for you, including times.
Work out how long you spent eating, playing, in different
lessons, and anything else important.

Quadrilaterals

To complete this unit, you have to understand
the following terms:

equal   the same length
opposite   on the other side
parallel   lines that remain the same distance apart
right angle a 'square' angle of 90°

parallel

parallel

parallel

Copy each of these quadrilaterals and name them.
Some have more than one name.
Use these definitions to help you decide:

with right angles

a rectangle has two pairs of parallel
sides

a square is a rectangle with all four
sides equal

without right angles

a rhombus has four equal, parallel
sides

a parallelogram has two pairs of
parallel sides

with or without a trapezium has one pair of sides equal

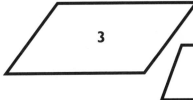

1   2   3   4   5

6 Mark all the right angles like this.

Draw some more quadrilaterals as follows, making them all different.

7 two trapezia
8 two parallelograms
9 one rhombus
10 three rectangles

Challenge

Draw some more shapes, but only using right angles (90°) and $\frac{1}{2}$ right angle (45°).

Triangles

To complete this unit, you have to recognise the following types of triangle:

equilateral triangle   all three sides are equal, and all three angles are equal (60°)

isosceles triangle   two sides are equal and two angles are equal

scalene triangle   all three sides are different and all three angles are different

right-angled triangle   one of the angles is a right angle, two sides **might** be equal and the other two angles **might** be equal

Carefully copy each of these triangles on squared paper. By the side of each write if it is equilateral, isosceles, scalene and/or right-angled. Some of the triangles can be more than one type.

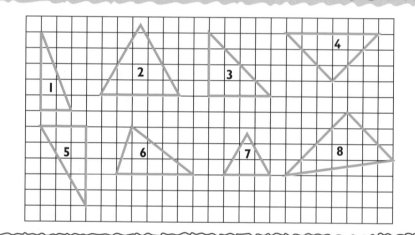

Draw some more triangles of your own that fit these descriptions.

9 a right-angled, isosceles triangle

10 a scalene triangle with one side 5 cm long and one side 7 cm long.

11 an equilateral triangle with sides 5 cm long.

12 an equilateral triangle with sides 6 cm long.

13 a right-angled scalene triangle with one side 3cm, one side 4cm and one side 5 cm

14 an isosceles triangle without a right angle

Challenge

Draw and cut out right-angled isosceles triangles. (A quick way to do this is to cut out squares and then cut them in two diagonally.)
See if they will fit together without leaving gaps.

Polyhedra

A polyhedron is a solid shape made up of flat faces. The number and shape of the faces helps us to recognise what sort it is. Here are some questions that will help you to identify a polyhedron:

- If it has 6 rectangular faces, it is a cube (if they are square faces) or a cuboid (if they are not square)
- If it is the same shape and size all the way through, so that the cross-sections are the same as the original shape, it is a prism — what type of prism depends on what shape the two ends are.
- If it has a flat base and a point at the top, it is pyramid. Pyramids are named after the shape of their base. If the bases is a circle, we call the shape a cone.

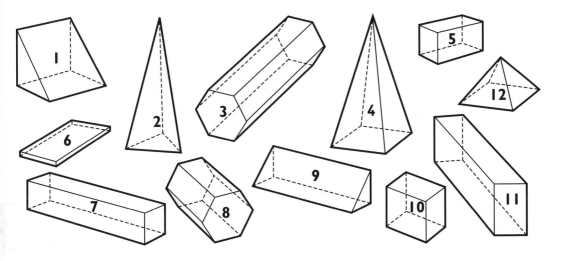

Make 3-D drawings of the following polyhedra.

13 a cube

14 a cuboid with a square face at each end (a square prism)

15 a pentagonal prism

Challenge

Make a list of as many things as you can that are cuboid.
Who can think of the most?

71

Unit 72
Line Symmetry

If a shape can be folded exactly in half, we say it is **symmetrical.** The line of the fold is called the **axis (or line) of symmetry**.
This shape has two axes of symmetry.
One half is a reflection of the other.
If you place a mirror down the line of symmetry, the shape will look complete.
We can make symmetrical patterns with objects like these by placing them on a grid.
Copy these patterns and draw in all the axes of symmetry.

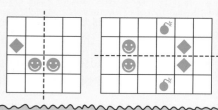

1

2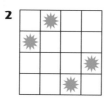

3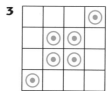

4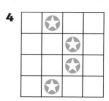

5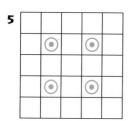

6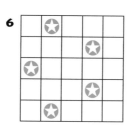

7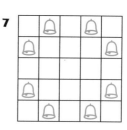

8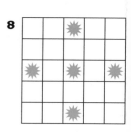

Now copy and complete the following patterns.

9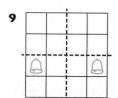

10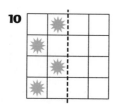

11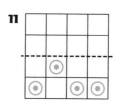

12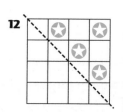

Challenge

Make up a symmetrical pattern of your own using an 8 × 8 square grid.

Translating and Rotating Shapes

This rectangle has been placed on a grid. It can be **translated** (moved) and it can be **rotated** (turned round).

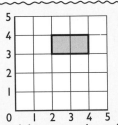 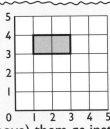 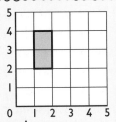

Draw these shapes on a grid, but translate (move) them as instructed.

1 Translate this shape one square to the left.

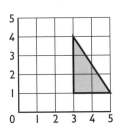

2 Translate this shape one square left and one square up.

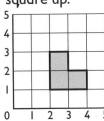

3 Translate this shape two squares right and one square down.

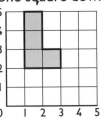

This shape has been rotated $\frac{1}{4}$ of a turn clockwise, around the point (3,2).

Draw these shapes, but rotate them (turn them around) as instructed.

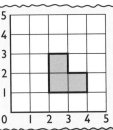 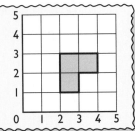

4 Rotate this rectangle $\frac{1}{2}$ a turn clockwise around (2, 3).

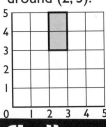

5 Rotate this rectangle $\frac{1}{4}$ a turn clockwise around (4, 2).

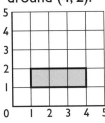

6 Rotate this square $\frac{1}{4}$ a turn clockwise around (2, 3).

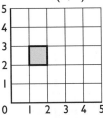

Challenge

Draw a grid on both large- and small-squared paper.
Cut out a shape, place it on the large-squared grid and draw it on the small-squared grid.
Rotate the cut-out shape and draw its new position on the grid, using a different colour.
Continue rotating and drawing until the shape is back in its original position.

Coordinates

We can mark positions on a grid using **coordinates**.
Two numbers are used, each one giving the position
in one direction.
The position in a **horizontal** direction is given
by the **x-axis**.
The position in a **vertical** direction is given by
the **y-axis**.
The area between these two axes is called the
first quadrant.
We always give the x-axis value first, then the y-axis value like this: (5, 2)

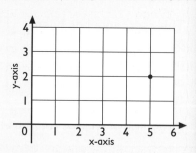

1 Write down the co-ordinates of the letters that are in the first quadrant below.

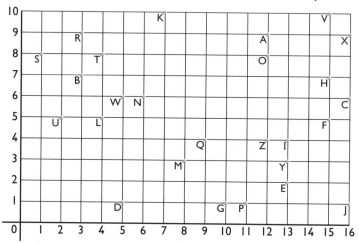

2 Copy the grid and mark the letters in these different positions:

A (13, 7)	**F** (16, 10)	**K** (15, 5)	**O** (9, 7)	**S** (4, 5)	**W** (13, 6)
B (4, 6)	**G** (2, 7)	**L** (13, 4)	**P** (3, 9)	**T** (4, 3)	**X** (10, 2)
C (1, 5)	**H** (5, 9)	**M** (14, 2)	**Q** (6, 7)	**U** (9, 5)	**Y** (8, 1)
D (10, 9)	**I** (12, 8)	**N** (1, 1)	**R** (4, 8)	**V** (11, 4)	**Z** (7, 0)
E (4, 2)	**J** (7, 5)				

Challenge

Try using one of these grids, or a grid of your own, to put a message into code.
Simply give the coordinates of the letters you want.
For spaces use a different 'empty' position each time, so that you can't tell how
many letters there are in each word.

Unit 75
Angles

When you use a protractor to measure an angle, it is very important to line it up correctly. Protractors usually have a scale numbered in both directions, so make sure you read the scale that starts at 0. If you are reading off the scale printed on the inside of the protractor, you can still use the outer scale's one-degree markings.

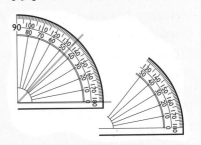

Before you measure, estimate: Is it close to, more than, or less than, a right angle (90°)?
Is it close to, more or less than half a right angle (45°)?

When you measure: Is your reading near your estimate? If not, have you read the correct scale?

1 Estimate then measure these angles.

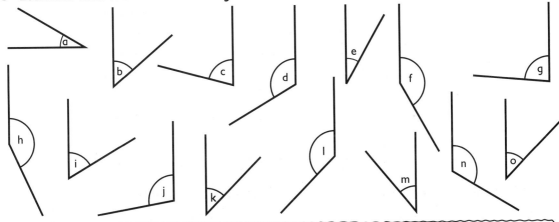

If an angle is **less than 90°**, we say it is **acute**. If it is **more than 90°** we say it is **obtuse**. We can usually tell by just looking.

2 Now look at the angles drawn above. Decide, just by looking, if they are acute or obtuse.

Challenge

Draw a few angles of your own.
With a partner, each estimate your angles.
Then measure to see how close you both were.

Unit 76
Angles on a Straight Line

Here is a horizontal line with a second line
perpendicular to it, making two right angles.
One of the two right angles has been marked
with a ☐ One right angle measures 90°,
so two together must equal 180°.
If we tilt the perpendicular line over, one of
the angles will become smaller and the other
will become bigger. Angles like these that are on
a straight line always add up to 180°.
When we know one angle, we can subtract it
from 180° to find the other angle.

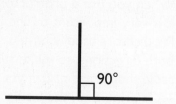

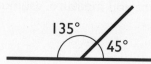

For each of these pairs of angles,
(a) measure the one marked (a)
(b) calculate the angle marked by subtracting angle (a) from 180°

Example   180° − 45° = 135°.

1

4
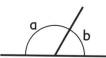

7

10
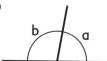

2

5

8
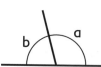

11
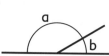

3

6
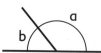

9

12
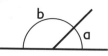

Challenge

Draw a few pairs of angles on a straight line. With a partner, both of you estimate
each angle.

76

Problems 13

1 Draw parallelograms that have:
   (a) 2 angles of 45°, 2 sides of 8 cm
      and 2 sides of 10 cm
   (b) 3 angles of 60°, 2 sides of 5 cm
      and 2 sides of 12 cm
   (c) 4 angles of 35°, 2 sides of 10 cm
      and 2 sides of 8 cm
   (d) 5 angles of 75°, 2 sides of 4 cm
      and 2 sides of 14 cm
   (e) 6 angles of 25°, 2 sides of 2 cm
      and 2 sides of 12 cm.

2 Draw shapes that match these descriptions:
   (a) a symmetrical triangle with one right angle
   (b) a symmetrical pentagon with three right angles
   (c) a pentagon with every line and angle different
   (d) a triangular prism with right-angled triangular faces at each end.

3 (a) Draw a grid 16 squares wide and 12 squares tall.
   (b) Label the x-axis 0 to 16 and the y-axis 0 to 12.
   (c) Drawing only along the grid lines, make a simple picture or design.
   (d) Using coordinates, write instructions for a partner who has not
      seen your design.
   (e) Swap instructions with a partner. Each of you try to draw the
      other's design just from the written instructions.
   (g) Check to see if both versions of each design look the same.
   (h) If there are differences, check through the instructions together.